W9-BEX-027

101 Ways to Score Higher on Your GRE:

What You Need to Know About the Graduate Record Exam Explained Simply

By Angela Eward-Mangione

101 Ways to Score Higher on Your GRE: What You Need to Know About the Graduate Record Exam Explained Simply

Copyright © 2009 by Atlantic Publishing Group, Inc.
1405 SW 6th Ave. • Ocala, Florida 34471 • 800-814-1132 • 352-622-1875–Fax
Web site: www.atlantic-pub.com • E-mail: sales@atlantic-pub.com
SAN Number: 268-1250

ISBN-13: 978-1-60138-224-5   ISBN-10: 1-60138-224-3

Library of Congress Cataloging-in-Publication Data

Eward-Mangione, Angela, 1978-
  101 ways to score higher on your GRE : what you need to know about the graduate record exam explained simply / by Angela Eward-Mangione.
       p. cm.
  Includes bibliographical references and index.
  ISBN-13: 978-1-60138-224-5 (alk. paper)
  ISBN-10: 1-60138-224-3 (alk. paper)
  1. Graduate Record Examination--Study guides. I. Title. II. Title: One hundred one ways to score higher on your GRE. III. Title: One hundred and one ways to score higher on your GRE.
  LB2367.4.E96 2009
  378.1'662--dc22
                    2008035791

Printed in the United States
PROJECT MANAGER: Melissa Peterson • mpeterson@atlantic-pub.com
INTERIOR DESIGN: Nicole Deck • ndeck@atlantic-pub.com

We recently lost our beloved pet "Bear," who was not only our best and dearest friend but also the "Vice President of Sunshine" here at Atlantic Publishing. He did not receive a salary but worked tirelessly 24 hours a day to please his parents. Bear was a rescue dog that turned around and showered myself, my wife Sherri, his grandparents Jean, Bob and Nancy and every person and animal he met (maybe not rabbits) with friendship and love. He made a lot of people smile every day.

We wanted you to know that a portion of the profits of this book will be donated to The Humane Society of the United States. *–Douglas & Sherri Brown*

The human-animal bond is as old as human history. We cherish our animal companions for their unconditional affection and acceptance. We feel a thrill when we glimpse wild creatures in their natural habitat or in our own backyard.

Unfortunately, the human-animal bond has at times been weakened. Humans have exploited some animal species to the point of extinction.

The Humane Society of the United States makes a difference in the lives of animals here at home and worldwide. The HSUS is dedicated to creating a world where our relationship with animals is guided by compassion. We seek a truly humane society in which animals are respected for their intrinsic value, and where the human-animal bond is strong.

Want to help animals? We have plenty of suggestions. Adopt a pet from a local shelter, or join The Humane Society and be a part of our work to help companion animals and wildlife. You will be funding our educational, legislative, investigative and outreach projects in the U.S. and across the globe.

Or perhaps you'd like to make a memorial donation in honor of a pet, friend or relative? You can through our Kindred Spirits program. And if you'd like to contribute in a more structured way, our Planned Giving Office has suggestions about estate planning, annuities, and even gifts of stock that avoid capital gains taxes.

Maybe you have land that you would like to preserve as a lasting habitat for wildlife. Our Wildlife Land Trust can help you. Perhaps the land you want to share is a backyard— that's enough. Our Urban Wildlife Sanctuary Program will show you how to create a habitat for your wild neighbors.

So you see, it's easy to help animals. And The HSUS is here to help.

THE HUMANE SOCIETY OF THE UNITED STATES.

2100 L Street NW • Washington, DC 20037 • 202-452-1100
www.hsus.org

Acknowledgements

First and foremost, I thank my husband, life partner, best friend and constant companion, Stephen Mangione. No matter what project I decide to engage in, he always fully supports me. Moreover, he trumps me in philosophical debates any day and can frequently outwit and out-write me. Thank you, Steve.

I also thank Paul Linn for his extensive support, encouragement, and direction. He has affected and changed my life in positive ways that exceed the scope of words.

Thank you also to Dr. Jim Lee from the University of Tampa for your exemplary integrity and advice. I also thank Dr. Sara Deats, Dr. Sylvia Fiore, and Dr. William Morris from the English Department at the University of South Florida.

Many other people have also touched my life in a profound and personal way: George Northrup, MD; Peter Walton, MD; Robert Casanas, MD, MA; Matthew Flickstein; Robert Theobald, MD; Ken Donaldson, MA; Fred Eppsteiner; Todd Yonteck, MD; Mark Milligan; Charles Lawrence Allen, MA; Dawn Balusik, AP, DOM, LMT; Minesh Patel, Ph.D.; Steve Shealy, Ph.D.; Keith and Cindi Matter; Nelson, Karol, Chris and Tiffany Mangione; Sylvia Mangione; Dr. Michael Garko; Neil Habgood; Russ and Christina Maynard; Lila Potter; Matt Cherry; Mark Mann; Jim Thigpen; Sandra Koch; Kenia Shaw; Lianne Potter; Robert Wilkerson; Reginald McGregor; Travis Monday; and Gary Stearns.

I also thank everyone who contributed a case study or interview to my book or who simply supported me during the process. Of course I must also thank ETS®. Thank you for creating the GRE®, providing the extensive support that you offer to students, and for consistently accepting feedback and making modifications to the test, as appropriate.

Table of Contents

CHAPTER 11: HOW TO PREPARE FOR THE ANALYTICAL WRITING SECTION OF THE GRE   227

CHAPTER 12: WHAT TO DO ONE WEEK BEFORE THE EXAM   241

CHAPTER 13: WHAT TO DO THE NIGHT BEFORE THE EXAM   247

CHAPTER 14: HOW TO HANDLE TEST DAY   251

CHAPTER 15: WHAT TO DO AFTER THE TEST   257

Foreword

101 Ways to Score Higher on Your GRE is much more than a study guide. It serves as your own personal coach through the graduate school and GRE preparation process.

No doubt you have picked up this book because you are, or someone you know is, thinking about graduate school. As a veteran GRE, LSAT®, and GMAT® test prep instructor and admissions coach, I am very familiar with the questions that plague students. Not only is the GRE looming above their heads, but so are much larger questions, such as figuring out which schools to apply to, when to take the GRE, how to deal with test anxiety, and even the much more basic question as to whether graduate school is the right decision for them.

I recommend this book with confidence to a wide range of students because author Angela Eward-Mangione takes a holistic approach towards the GRE test preparation journey. *101 Ways to Score Higher on Your GRE* places your GRE score within the context of your overall admissions plan and professional goals. In case you are still hazy about what you want to do with your life, this book offers several challenging questions so that you can develop a well-thought-out plan and make educated decisions about whether applying to graduate school is the right thing for you to do and, if so, which fields and graduate programs you should apply to.

Then, once you have a vision for your future and have committed to taking the GRE, this book leads you through the often complicated application process by offering solid advice in crafting your overall application package.

Are you unsure about what to include in your personal statement? This book will get you brainstorming about your goals so that the task of writing an application essay is no longer so daunting.

And, of course, *101 Ways to Score Higher on Your GRE* provides an excellent overview of how to prepare for the GRE. You will find strategies for each question type and a handy GRE vocabulary list, as well as some commonly-tested concepts and tried-and-true strategies to tackle the math section. This section is an excellent jump-start to preparing for the GRE and should be used as a companion guide to a more detailed quantitative and verbal review.

A fantastic feature of the book is the chapter on reducing test anxiety. Getting in the right frame of mind is often overlooked by students who are already overwhelmed by the prospect of taking the GRE and the application process in general. This book not only provides a blueprint for organizing your application and the GRE preparation process, but it also gives you a brief do-it-yourself anxiety reduction method to put you in the right frame of mind so that you can get started right away.

Finally, *101 Ways to Score Higher on Your GRE* is written from a first-person perspective with anecdotes about preparing for and taking the GRE, with case studies from invited contributors. Many people who study on their own feel as if their journey in GRE prep is an isolated one, but this book provides camaraderie so that the process of studying for the GRE is a fun challenge rather than a daunting obstacle.

As a managing member of the Washington, D.C.-based Test Heads Educational Coaching, LLC and as a test prep instructor in the business since 1998, I have seen over one thousand GRE, GMAT®, and LSAT® students forge ahead in test preparation. More than half of our students have already taken a course with one of those 'Big Name' companies and they come seeking assistance that will work. A great number of other students have sought to self-study, but don't know where to start. Either way, one of our biggest responsibilities at Test Heads is to make the most out of our time with students and to recommend resources that will help guide students through the process of the GRE preparation and graduate school application process. Many tutoring and group instruction hours could be enhanced with *101 Ways to Score Higher on Your GRE*, and I look forward to integrating this book into our test preparation courses.

Theresa Gheen (JD, LLM), Managing Member
Test Heads Educational Coaching, LLC.
www.testheads.com
Washington, DC

Preface

All GRE (Graduate Record Exam) prep books are alike - except for this one. When you cruise the Internet or bookstore shelves for books on how to prepare for the GRE, you will find that a sea of books with nearly identical structures and substance awaits you. There is nothing wrong with any of these books. Many of them may serve as an excellent companion to this book. What these books lack, though, is a holistic approach that addresses every aspect of the GRE process — from the decision of actually entering graduate school, all the way to what to do after reaching the finish line on test day. Moreover, none of the GRE prep books on the market express any advice or sentiments from a personal point of view. No interviews with professors pop off the page. No case studies of past test takers are included. No advice from medical and mental health professionals on how to calm your nerves is offered. More important, no author speaks from the voice of personal experience.

The GRE is administered by the ETS® (Educational Testing Service). Currently, ETS® is the world's largest private testing and measurement organization. ETS® develops several tests besides the GRE, including:

- SAT® (formerly Scholastic Aptitude Test)

- PSAT/NMSQT® (Preliminary SAT/National Merit Scholarship Qualifying Test)

- CLEP® (College Level Examination Program)

- TOEFL® (Test of English as a Foreign Language)

- TOEIC® (Test of English for International Communications)

- TFI (Test de Francais International)

- CAHSEE (California High School Exit Exam)

- Praxis Test (formerly NTE)

Incidentally, ETS® is a non-profit organization, and therefore exempt from paying federal income tax. Essentially, ETS® is exclusively focused on developing tests and implementing test-taking and scoring standards. ETS® will not view you or your scores as individual or personalized. You will simply be a numbered test taker to ETS®; your scores are just numbers to them as well. Along those lines, the GRE has been criticized for serving as more of a measure of how well a person can perform on a standardized test than his or her actual intellectual capability, let alone one's likelihood of success in the first year of graduate school. The future of the GRE is uncertain. In 2006, ETS® responded to criticism directed at the GRE with a promise to revamp the entire test. Those plans were later dropped. ETS® has decided, instead, to make slow and gradual changes to the general GRE test. This book anticipates those changes by addressing the few that have already taken place, which you may or may not even encounter on your test day.

I decided to write *101 Ways to Score Higher on the GRE: What You Need to Know About Your Graduate Record Exam Explained Simply* because I wanted to give test takers a useful and unique option to utilize in their preparations for this exam. Again, every GRE prep book on the market will give you test-taking strategies. They will also provide plenty of practice questions. Each book will teach you about the scoring system and how to win. These aspects of the GRE are extremely important, if not entirely critical, and are therefore included in this book as well. This book, though, gives you more than the average GRE prep book. This book will challenge you to think about why you are taking the GRE. It will compel you to make decisions about which schools and programs to which you wish to send your graduate studies application. You will examine your "life purpose," mission, and vision and clearly decide how taking the GRE aligns with that purpose. This deep examination will renew your commitment to graduate studies, which will invigorate your commitment to score well on the GRE. Prior to even beginning to study for the GRE, you will also choose and begin an anxiety and nerve controlling technique. Some people will choose to begin a meditation practice. Others will opt to do some imagery work every day. Everyone's choice will be different. Whatever choice you make, your anxiety aiding strategy, when practiced regularly, will assist you up to and including test day. Next, you will delve into the scoring system and test taking strategies. You will quickly learn that practice truly can make perfect, and so can studying. Another unique quality about this book is that it will not just throw a vocabulary list at you along with some practice algebra or geometry questions. This book will teach you the organizational and time management skills necessary to commence a monumental studying process. You will develop your own, unique study schedule. Then, you will study. You will also practice; then, you will practice, practice, and practice some more. You will learn about some of the changes that ETS® (Educational Testing Service) made to the GRE, effective November of 2007. These changes—the addition of two new types of questions—may or may not affect you. You may receive a section with a new question type, and you may not. Either way, you will be prepared. This book does not abandon you after the preparation work and practice problems. You will be guided all the way up to, including and after your test day. You will learn how to handle the week before your exam. You will also consider what you might wish to do (or not do) the night prior to your GRE test date. You will know what to do when test day comes; you will be armed with plenty of strategies, along with the anxiety controlling technique that you have been practicing regularly all along. Finally, you will take your GRE. Even then, you will not find yourself forsaken. This book contains suggestions—from first-hand experience—about what to do immediately after taking your test. You will also learn how to handle the possibility of being dissatisfied with your scores. All these aspects make this book entirely unique.

Be sure to take note of the vocabulary list in Chapter 9, and also the mathematical—algebraic and geometrical—formulas in Chapter 10. Buy yourself index cards and make flashcards if you find that helpful. You may also find flashcards on the market that could serve as an excellent complement to this book. Moreover, this book provides you with plenty of other resources that can assist you with your GRE preparation process. Again, you will not simply work through a myriad of questions and strategies and then find yourself abandoned. You will be guided every step of the way: from your dream seedling within the acorn of your life vision and purpose, all the way to and beyond the finish line on test day.

I would like to offer one final comment to future test takers. Rather than talk to you from an depersonalized voice and simply encourage you to read this book and do all the practice problems, I would like to invite you to use this opportunity to find the courage and determination deep within yourself that will allow you to succeed on this test and subsequently become the man or woman you deserve to become. Whatever you do, do not begin this process pessimistically. If you have heard nightmare stories about the GRE, forget about them. Actually, when I approached professionals about contributing case studies and interviews for this book, many of them had a negative reaction just from hearing the word "GRE." The GRE is just a test, and nothing more than a test; never forget that. Pretend like you are a track runner about to embark on a marathon. If you are taking the test tomorrow, we cannot do much training together; you must sprint. Eat a power bar and get ready to run as fast as you possibly can. If you are taking the test in a few weeks, you will need to run fast. But at least you have a marginally reasonable amount of time to scan every one of the 101 strategies and tips in this book and go through a few practice sets of test questions. If you have at least a month before your GRE test date, congratulations; we have got some time to work and train together. Better yet, if you have at least two to three months before you take the GRE, prepare for a fascinating, fun, and festive marathon. Remember, though, it is just a test. It is like a marathon, which is difficult, but doable. Do not make this more than it is. You just need to train before race, or "test," day arrives. I ran my first marathon in May 2008. It seemed daunting at first: the prospect of running a 5K race. "What if I cannot do it?" I asked myself at the time. After only a week of training, I was able to run 3.11 miles (5K) in 28 minutes. I worked hard to achieve this and you will also need to put considerable time and effort into your GRE studies.

This is *your* race. It is *your* marathon. It is *your* life. So *you* decide how *you* want to run *your* race. *You* decide how to pace your marathon. *You* decide what to do with *your* life. Remember, though, that as painstaking as marathons can be, the exhilaration of crossing the finish line cannot be compared to any other experience on this earth. Sure, you will encounter challenges on the way. You will get tired and thirsty, and you may even want to quit. Conversely, you can fully expect to encounter unexpected delights. You will feel the anticipation throughout your training, and then perhaps even enjoy the exhilaration of race day.

So, put on your track shoes, pace yourself, and prepare for a long run. Go for the Gold.

Good luck.

Introduction

A quick glance at the GRE Web site, **www.greguide.com**, reveals that the GRE is a standardized test administered and directed by The Educational Testing Service (ETS®), and used by graduate schools in many parts of the world to determine whether an applicant is likely to succeed in graduate studies. The last point is debatable; many academics and laymen alike argue that the GRE is more effective at measuring how well one can score on a standardized test rather than how successful he or she can be in graduate school.

Nonetheless, the GRE, or Graduate Record Exam, consists of two versions: the general exam and 12 different subject exams. Far more graduate schools require the general exam than any one of the subject area exams, and this guide is designed to prepare you for success on the general exam, which tests abstract thinking skills in verbal reasoning, mathematics, and written expression. The scores provide a common measure for comparing the abilities of the applicants in each of these three areas.

HOW IS THE GRE USED?

Recent admissions to the graduate school of political science at Florida State University (FSU) can be used to illustrate how graduate schools use GRE scores. The FSU graduate program in political science maintains minimum admission requirements of combined quantitative and verbal scores on the

GRE of 1100 with no less than 500 on either of those sections, and a grade point average (GPA) of 3.0 during the last two years of coursework. Yet, students who were actually admitted to the program in 2007-08 had GPAs of 3.25 to 3.90 and had a combined score of over 1252 on the quantitative and verbal sections of the GRE. The FSU Web site specifically states, "We purposefully limit the number of students we accept to ensure that each student gets the personal attention they deserve in a high quality Ph.D. program . . . [so] meeting the minimum requirements for GRE and GPA is not a guarantee of admission."

Furthermore, for those students seeking financial support from the graduate school of their choice, GRE scores may be a determining factor in receiving such support. The University of California at Irvine states that although there is no minimum score requirement to receive fellowships, fellowships are rarely awarded in the absence of a complete application packet, including GRE scores.

GENERAL FACTS ABOUT THE GRE

1. The GRE is a standardized test.

2. There are two forms of the GRE: the general knowledge test and 12 subject area tests.

3. Most colleges and universities require the general knowledge test.

4. A few colleges and universities, or particular programs within them, require a subject area exam.

5. The general knowledge test has three scored sections: verbal reasoning, mathematical skills, and written expression.

6. GRE ® scores may affect your ability to receive financial aid or the amount of aid that is offered.

7. A high score on the GRE ® is not a guarantee of admission to the college, university, or program of your choice.

THE STRUCTURE OF THE GRE

Earning high scores on the GRE depends somewhat on understanding the structure of the exam. The exam is a standardized test; that is, the questions are written specifically to measure the abilities of a particular group, in this case, college students. Before the exam can be used in an official sense, the questions are "normed" by trying them out on a group of people who are strikingly similar to future test takers. If the questions meet the requirements of validity and reliability, they can then be used in the formal test taking situation.

Validity involves systematic examination of the test content or questions to determine whether the questions cover a representative sample of the information being measured. Each question is chosen to comply with a test specification or plan regarding the subject matter of the test. A panel of experts may be used to review the test specifications and the questions to determine whether they are valid, or whether the questions need revision. So, long before you take the GRE, a number of other people with expertise in the content areas and expertise in designing standardized tests have analyzed your test to make sure that it measures what it is intended to measure.

Reliability, on the other hand, is a much simpler concept. It means that the test questions provide a consistent measurement over time and repeated usage in the same conditions. A test can be reliable without being valid, that is, the measurement can be the same time after time without necessarily being "right."

The third standard the GRE (and other standardized tests) must meet is creating a bell curve when a group of test takers' scores are plotted on a graph. The scores of the large majority of the test takers will fall in the middle of all possible scores, with a few people's scores falling at either end of the curve as low or extremely high scores.

According to the curriculum of any undergraduate psychometrics course, all this boils down to predictability. In order for the GRE to be a standardized test, it must be extremely predictable. It is this predictability that allows colleges and universities to make value judgments about student performance based on GRE scores, and it is the predictability that allows you to "learn" how to take the test. Thank goodness for predictability!

If you have a bad attitude about taking standardized tests, it is time to change it. Look at the GRE as a puzzle that you can figure out. Not only can you figure it out, but it can be fun and rewarding to do so. The first important point to remember is that the GRE tests "concepts." Every question on the test is actually asking for the same information over and over again. If you look at the math questions, all of them are testing the same mathematical concepts. If you look at the vocabulary items, the same ones occur over and over again in the various forms of the test. Like many puzzles, once you have this key information in place, the rest of the puzzle is easier to solve.

Prior to embarking on your GRE general test preparation and training program, it would be wise for you consider your motivation for taking the test. Are you committed to a certain career? Is that career an academic career? Do you want to get a graduate degree to learn research and writing skills? Or, is it possible that you just do not know what else to do with your life and so you have decided to enter graduate school? Taking the GRE is not cheap; it will cost you $140 each time. Moreover, sitting through the GRE exam is not a particularly relaxing way to spend a morning or afternoon. You will be better served if you take some time to examine your motivation for taking this test. Doing so will boost your confidence and score.

◆ **CHAPTER 1**

Considering Why You
Want a Graduate Degree

Tip #1: Consider your life's purpose/mission.

Does getting a graduate degree truly fit into your life's mission? If so, get ready to rock and prepare for the GRE. If not, why torture yourself? If you have a valid reason for wanting to obtain a graduate degree, you will indeed need to take the GRE. Though, prior to putting yourself through the considerable time and effort necessary to prepare for and take the GRE, make sure that you know why you are taking this exam, why you want to go to graduate school, and what you intend to do with your graduate degree.

There is nothing more important in life than discovering your life purpose; not even taking the GRE trumps this feat. If you do not know your purpose in life, you may end up living according to the dreams and expectations of others. Understandably, if you are reading this book and find yourself in your early 20s, you may find it difficult or impossible to clearly identify your life purpose. You might, though, have some idea of what you are here to do.

The idea of having a "life purpose" is perhaps debatable. "How do you know I have a life purpose?" you might ask—and rightfully so. To be honest and straightforward with you, there is no clear and hard cut evidence that I can present to convince you that your life has a purpose. I am simply incapable of producing anything tangible which directly points to the existence of a "life purpose" for anyone. This question, "What is my life purpose?" is somewhat similar to the, "What is the meaning of life?" question. These questions are astute, yet abstract, daunting yet daring, and require both guts and gumption to fully face and answer. Philosophically speaking, one might argue that life has no purpose. Factor common sense into this equation, though. What has compelled you to read this book? Did you just randomly pick it up? Why did you obtain an undergraduate degree? What about going to graduate school interests you? Why are you not watching television or playing video games instead of reading this book? Clearly, the answers to these questions point to something intangible yet identifiable and recognizable. There are reasons for our behavior. Something has motivated you to take the GRE. Something has motivated you to pursue graduate studies. This has to do with your life purpose.

CASE STUDY: KENILEE INC.

10410 Seminole Blvd., #3
Seminole, FL 33778
(727) 394-7325
www.realationshipcoach.com
Ken Donaldson, M.A., LMHC - The REALationship
Life Coach

What is the Purpose of My Life? Living Your Life on Purpose.

We each have a unique purpose. We are here for a significant reason. When you know what that is and you live according to it, you will experience the passion of living your purpose, and you will have an amazingly positive impact on humankind.

When it comes to discovering your life purpose, answer the following for yourself. Get a pen and some paper and write down your answers as best as you can, spontaneously, right now.

- What is it that turns me on?

- What is my unique gift or talent?

CASE STUDY: KENILEE INC.

- What do I do, or have wanted to do, that would make a huge difference in the world today?

- What is it that I do that gives my life meaning?

- What do I most look forward to doing? What makes the activity so enjoyable?

- Where am I happiest? What about that place makes me so happy?

- If I had $1,000,000,000 (Yes, that is one billion dollars!) to spend on one cause, what would I spend it on? What about that cause is worth investing in?

- If I were to describe my ideal or perfect day, what would it look like, sound like and be like?

Go back and look at what you have written here. What are the common threads that keep showing up? What is the fire in your belly that wakes you up in the middle of the night? Work with this process until you come up with the completed statement, *"The purpose of my life is _____."* Do not stop until that statement resonates as a 10 on a scale from 1 to 10, with 10 having the highest level of resonance.

Copyright @ 2005 Ken Donaldson

Marry Yourself First! Saying "I Do" to a Life of Passion, Power & Purpose."

Gaining clarity about your life purpose before you take the GRE, enter graduate school and make all the significant sacrifices that go along with those actions will undoubtedly benefit you. Those who discover that their purpose in life is to be a college or university professor, or teacher, may benefit from a graduate degree. Those who wish to advance their careers may also benefit from a graduate degree. Even so, those who are unclear about their life's purpose may also benefit from a graduate degree, because obtaining one may help them narrow down what they are and are not interested in, particularly in terms of academics. Conversely, if you feel that your purpose in life is to spend your time being a scuba diving instructor or chef, why bother taking the GRE?

Tip #2: Decide if you want to become a college or university professor.

If you are certain that you would like to become a college or university Professor, there is absolutely no doubt as to whether you will need to take the GRE. If this is your chosen career route, you will need to do more than simply take the GRE. You will need to score as highly as possible, as this will put you in a better position to receive scholarships or fellowships. Also, take note: You will want to become a recognized expert in your field. Competition may accelerate. As discussed earlier, having a high GRE score may earn you scholarships and endowments, all of which will look excellent on your Curriculum Vitae (CV) or résumé.

You should also know the following: If you wish to teach in a community college, you will need at least a Master's degree. Many community colleges prefer to hire candidates with a Ph.D. or applicants currently working on the completion of a Ph.D. Your GRE scores may not be a factor in the interviewing process for a teaching position at a community college. Your GRE scores, on the other hand, will affect whether you can enter the graduate program of your choice and subsequently secure a teaching position at the community college of your choice. Also, if you do achieve excellent scores on the GRE, this may serve you well in the interview process at a community college. Since I scored a perfect 6.0 on the analytical writing section of the GRE, I made that aspect of my résumé and credentials front and center when I applied for jobs at colleges. It also served me well when I applied to be a Ph.D. candidate in the field of my choice.

As for universities, some will hire applicants with a Master's degree. This would occur, though, on a case-by-case basis and would only likely apply to candidates with exceptional backgrounds and credentials. You are more likely to be considered for a position if you are currently pursuing a Ph.D. Most universities, though, require a Ph.D. to apply for full-time, tenured faculty positions. Also, GRE scoring requirements for a Master's degree program may differ for Ph.D. programs. This is a point you must absolutely investigate before taking the GRE because select universities only admit candidates who intend to acquire a Ph.D. You must consider these points (whether you wish to pursue an M.A. or Ph.D degree and what the GRE score requirements are for each degree) before you take the GRE.

Tip #3: Decide if you currently work in a field in which procuring a graduate degree might help you earn more money.

Those who do not wish to obtain a graduate degree for professional reasons may benefit from a good, solid graduate education. Graduate school teaches individuals many valuable tools and skills, including researching, writing, project management, organization, time management, determination, fortitude, and communication skills.

One reason that you might wish to earn a graduate degree (and therefore need to take the GRE) is to earn more money in your field. For example, most teachers in the public school system earn more money on an annual basis if they have a Master's degree, as opposed to a bachelor's degree. A writer who procures a graduate degree in nearly any subject will obtain the research and writing skills necessary to take his or her career to the next level. This may result in increased earnings; it did for me. Moreover, anyone who obtains at least a Master's degree in his or her field of study becomes eligible to teach on the community college level. Those who procure a Ph.D. may teach at a university, depending on their other credentials, background, and scholarship record. This opens up additional opportunities for income. One could have a full-time job during the day and teach at a community college or university in the evening for extra money.

CASE STUDY: ANGELA EWARD-MANGIONE, M.L.A

Tampa, Florida
813-966-6301
www.writers.net/writers/24800
Angela Eward-Mangione, M.L.A. – Freelance
Author, Writer, Editor

Earning More Money with a Graduate Degree

When I completed my bachelor's degree, I worked at a less than satisfying job within a large hotel chain. My bachelor's degree was in English. I knew that I wanted to pursue a graduate degree, but did not feel 100 percent certain about what applications might interest me. I had an interest in teaching on the college level. I also, however, had an interest in, and a talent for, writing. Part of me also simply yearned to learn more.

Ultimately, I decided to pursue a graduate degree to increase my education, hone my organization skills, explore the possibilities of college and/or University teaching and to improve my writing skills. My life-long dream was to become a writer, but I also had an interest in college or university level teaching.

Now, when I look back and compare my writing from when I first completed my bachelor's degree with after I had completed my Master's degree, I am awestruck and amazed. The contrast can be likened to night and day — literally. Moreover, after completing a bachelor's degree in English, I had little to no writing gigs or opportunities waiting in the wings, so to speak. The best I could hope for at that point, in terms of a professional career, was a string of $10-11 hour jobs at various companies. I thought perhaps I could find work as a proofreader or newspaper assistant.

Completing a Master's degree increased my writing and organization skills exponentially. Taking graduate level courses worked my brain. Writing graduate-level papers demanded more of me than writing bachelor's-level papers had. I needed to visit the library more frequently. I procured a thesaurus! I received some tutoring in writing. Moreover, the editing and writing advice I received during my thesis writing process was valuable.

As a result, I launched my career as a freelance writer and editor during my third year of graduate school. I had my first customer within two

CASE STUDY: ANGELA EWARD-MANGIONE, M.L.A

months. A year later, I had three customers. The following year, I had a total of nine customers; my earnings as a "freelancer" had reached a full-time level. None of this would have happened if I had not pursued a graduate degree.

I am currently deciding whether to incorporate. I may soon be a business owner! If not, I will always be a successful freelance author, writer and editor due to my decision to pursue a graduate level degree.

Also, pursuing a Master's degree to earn more money would be more common than pursuing a Ph.D. for these reasons. There are few cases in which a student might pursue and complete a Ph.D. to increase his or her annual salary. Middle and high school teachers with a Ph.D. are compensated with additional wages above and beyond those with a master's or bachelor's degree. Community college teachers who have a Ph.D. earn more money than their master's level colleagues. Other than that, there are few reasons for a student to actively pursue a Ph.D. for monetary reasons.

CASE STUDY: MARTIN SCHÖNFELD, PH.D.

4202 E Fowler Avenue, FAO 226
Tampa, Florida 33620
813-974-5914
www.cas.usf.edu/philosophy/schonf
poetrybeingzen.blogspot.com/
Martin Schönfeld, Ph.D
Professor of Philosophy: The University
of South Florida

The Purpose of a Ph.D. in the Arts and Sciences

The Ph.D. is a degree in scientific or scholarly training. The ticket for success is to pursue a degree in scientific or scholarly training for the purpose of science or scholarship.

Pursuing a degree in scientific or scholarly training for non-scientific or non-scholarly reasons complicates the pursuit. In that case, the Ph.D. won't be an end anymore, but becomes a means for something else. Acquiring

CASE STUDY: MARTIN SCHÖNFELD, PH.D.

this tool requires so much energy, focus, and time that folks whose interests lay elsewhere (and thus do not take the Ph.D for what it is) tend to run out of steam.

Ask yourself whether the following helps:

Jeff and Jane are equally talented and both pursue a Ph.D. in math.

Jeff wants to get a Ph.D. in math because he wants to make a killing on the stock market.

Jane wants to get a Ph.D. in math because she wants to be a mathematician.

Every morning Jeff motivates himself for his math work by reminding himself of the carrot of big bucks dangling ahead of him in the future.

Jeff is not happy, but he hopes he'll be happening eight years hence.

Every morning Jane gets up and already is who she has always wanted to be. Jane is happy, and she's happening. Who stands better chances of seeing the pursuit of the Ph.D. all the way through — Jeff or Jane?

Tip #4: Decide if you want to procure a graduate degree for personal enhancement.

Pursuing a graduate degree for personal enhancement (as a hobby or "just for fun") is risky, but valid. Any reason that you have for wanting to do something is good enough. As I said in the preface, this is your life, not your mom's, dad's, friends' or anybody else's. You must simply make yourself aware of the time and financial investments that are required for your personal enhancement courses and degrees. Also, to obtain a graduate education from an accredited University, you may need to submit GRE scores. Be certain that you want to put forth the time and effort necessary to prepare for the GRE in order to gain acceptance into a graduate program for personal enhancement.

Technically, there are no "invalid" reasons for pursuing any graduate degree, whether it is a master's or Ph.D. degree. One might be ill-advised, however, to spend the time, effort and money involved without a definite, clear plan and understanding of why you want this degree. I do know people who have up to three higher level degrees. I know one woman who has two Ph.D.s and a law degree. She considers herself well-rounded and is satisfied with the choices she made in pursuing her heart's desires.

At the risk of sounding crass: follow your heart but use your brain. If you want a master's or Ph.D. degree, go get one. The world is your playground. Again, this is your life; you call the shots. Do not forget, however, that graduate degrees require time, money and sacrifice. As long as you are aware of and comfortable with these factors, go follow your dreams. Prior to take-off, though, do not forget that regardless of your reasons) for obtaining a graduate degree, you must earn your spot in a program. Your GRE scores will play a critical factor in that arena.

Tip #5: Make sure that you are not pursuing a graduate degree just because you do not want to grow up.

Unfortunately, many students pursue a graduate degree simply because they are not sure what else to do with their lives. Moreover, many students do not want to face the prospect of paying back hefty student loans and other debts they may have incurred as a student. I once met a student who entered a graduate program just so that he could delay the repayment of his student loans! Graduate school is hard work and requires time, effort and a significant personal commitment. It should not be taken lightly. Moreover, graduate school should not be entered simply because one is not sure what else to do with one's life. Unless you are a teacher's aide (TA) who receives tuition reimbursement, you must foot the bill for your graduate school education. Do not waste your time or money. If you are not sure what to do with your life, go to the career counseling center at your college or university while you are enrolled as a student. If you are not currently a student anywhere, there are many resources available on the web which may assist you. Additionally, you can check the self-help and career section(s) of any local bookstore to find more books on how to find your passion and purpose in life. I recommend the following, all of which had a significant impact on my life:

- *Marry YourSelf First: Saying "I Do" to a Life of Passion, Power and Purpose,* by Ken Donaldson

- *Change Your Life in 30 Days: A Journey to Finding Your True Self,* by Rhonda Britten

- *Zen and the Art of Making a Living: A Practical Guide to Creative Career Design,* by Laurence G. Boldt

CHAPTER 1 HOMEWORK

1. Complete the life purpose exercise, from page 22. Below is a reminder of the questions. When it comes to discovering your life purpose, answer the following for yourself. Get a pen and some paper and write down your answers as best as you can, spontaneously, right now.

- What is it that turns me on?

- What is my unique gift or talent?

- What do I do, or have wanted to do, that would make a huge difference in the world today?

- What is it that I do that gives my life meaning?

- What do I most look forward to doing? What makes the activity so enjoyable?

- Where am I happiest? What about that place makes me so happy?

- If I had $1,000,000,000 (Yes, that is one *billion* dollars!) to spend on one cause, what would I spend it on? What about that cause is worth investing in?

- If I were to describe my ideal or perfect day, what would it look like, sound like and be like?

Go back and look at what you have written here. What are the common threads that keep showing up? What is the *fire in your belly* that wakes you up in the middle of the night? Work with this process until you come up with the completed statement, "*The purpose of my life is* _____." Do not stop until that statement resonates as a 10 on a scale from 1 to 10, with 10 having the highest level of resonance.

2. Do you want to become a college or university professor? If you are not sure, you should interview two professors within the next week. Ask them what they like and dislike about teaching. Tell them about your background and educational experience and also discuss your career goals with them. You might also access your school or public library to find out the current salaries for part- and full-time college and university faculty. Make sure that you will be comfortable living off of these salaries.

3. Would procuring a graduate degree help you earn more money? What is your career field of interest? Check your school or local library, or use online resources to investigate if a higher education degree would add up to a higher pay check for you. For example, most high school teachers in the state of Florida earn an additional $3,000 per year for having a master's degree. Educators with a Ph.D. earn additional income as well.

4. If you are interested in a graduate degree for personal enhancement and self-development reasons, write a one paragraph statement about how you envision a graduate degree significantly changing your life. What aspects of your development will a graduate degree directly affect? Be prepared — people will ask you questions like, "What do you plan to do with your degree?" Are you prepared to tell people that you received your degree for personal development? If not, get ready. Take some time to think about this scenario (if it applies to you) and do some brief writing about it.

5. Write a three paragraph statement about how you are not procuring a graduate degree simply because you do not want to grow up. In the first paragraph, include a detailed explanation of why you intend to pursue this degree (this will be excellent practice for your admissions essay anyway). In the second paragraph, write about how you intend to utilize your graduate degree. In the third paragraph, write about the importance of financial responsibility, and how you are not pursuing a graduate degree to shirk debt or bill payments.

CHAPTER 2

Deciding Which Graduate Program You Wish to Enter

The first step in preparing for the GRE is deciding which program you plan to enter at a university. While this might seem premature, it is actually not. Some universities will have standard GRE requirements for graduate admissions. Other universities will defer GRE score requirements to the individual departments. In the latter case, departmental requirements may vary. For example, a graduate program in English may not care about your quantitative score but may require an exceptionally high verbal reasoning score. Conversely, an engineering program may be more concerned about the score you receive on the math section of your GRE and may not be overly eager to review your verbal or analytical writing score. By deciding which program you plan to enter ahead of time, you can research the program requirements and individualize and focus your GRE test preparation time.

I advise you to select the program you wish to enter before you select a school. Why? You are going to work hard at preparing for the GRE. After that, you will need to climb the mountain of the graduate admissions process. Moreover, this is all about pursuing your goals in life. It is preferable for you to enter the program of your choice. Not all universities will offer the program you wish to enter. Why waste your time getting the GRE admission requirements for a school that does not even offer the program you want? Conversely, what if you decide that you want to pursue a degree in transpersonal psychology and decide to attend a school that does not even require the GRE for the admissions process?

Please, save yourself the heartache of an ill-planned graduate school career and do your research ahead of time. It will not take long. Let's get started.

Tip #6: Clearly re-emphasize to yourself why you want a graduate degree.

You have already done good work in this area in the previous chapter. However, to hone in on the program you wish to enter (unless you already have a program in mind, for certain); you need to re-emphasize to yourself why you want a graduate degree. Here is a review of the possible reasons:

- You want to become a college or university teacher/professor

- You want to earn more money in your current field/profession

- You want to receive personal enhancement

- You do not want to grow up and face the real world of bills and responsibilities

CASE STUDY: AMY JORGENSEN

AJCopywriting – Co-owner and Head Copywriter

Evansville, Indiana

When I was working on my bachelor's degree in English at the University of Southern Indiana, I never thought about going on to graduate school. My plan was to become a high school English teacher and continue writing as a hobby in my free time. That plan fell apart when I realized I wasn't ready to teach teenagers and might never be ready.

CASE STUDY: AMY JORGENSEN

After graduating, I struggled to figure out what to do with my degree. Few jobs were available for writers in my city and those that were available required more experience than I had accumulated. My self-esteem plummeted because I couldn't find a job and even after I finally found a niche as an online freelance writer I always felt let down by myself and my education.

In 2005, my husband's job was outsourced so he decided to go back to college. That's when I decided it was time for me to take my education further as well. Working on my Master's degree required some sacrifices. I had to give up my job teaching at Indiana Business College because I couldn't juggle my freelance writing, teaching, and completing my coursework.

After finishing my Master's degree in December 2007, I can say the sacrifices were worth it. While earning the degree did finally allow me to achieve my dream of teaching at a university (I was hired to teach public speaking at my alma mater during my final semester), it was the courses and professors themselves that had the biggest impact on my life.

The challenges of the coursework required more work, but successfully earning high marks and praise from my professors boosted my self-esteem tremendously. Some of the courses forced me to re-evaluate my views and ended up changing the way I perceive the world for the better. Expanding what I know and gaining these new experiences also made me a more well-rounded and confident writer.

Additionally, my graduate work didn't just impact my life. Both my husband and daughter have been positively affected, too. I brought home my education, shared it with them, and inspired them to work harder and to pursue their own educational goals. I also inspired myself.

My next goal is to pursue my Ph.D. so I can secure a full-time position as a professor instead of working as just an adjunct. Before challenging myself to complete my master's degree, I would never have had the courage to set such a goal. Now I can look toward the start of that new segment of my education with excitement.

Tip #7: If you want to become a community college or university instructor, decide whether you are going to further your education in your field of study or if you are going to branch into a new (but perhaps related) field.

You must now decide whether you wish to further your education in your undergraduate field of study, or if you are going to pursue a graduate degree in a different field. Most people who want to become an instructor do further their current field. Some people do branch off into interdisciplinary work, though. For example, I received a bachelor's degree in English, but received a Master's degree in Liberal Arts, which was an interdisciplinary program in which I studied English, Philosophy, and Art History.

If you already have an idea of what school and program you wish to attend, congratulations; you are one step ahead of the game. If you are not sure what school you want to attend, you will want to begin this research process by choosing a program. You can then select a school. After you have completed those steps, you can check the admissions requirements for the school and program of your choice.

Below, find a list of graduate degree programs offered by several universities throughout the United States. If you have not yet chosen a program, this will help you begin brainstorming along those lines.

Accounting	Dentistry School (DDS)
Aerospace Engineering	Design: Media Arts
African Studies	Early Childhood Education
Afro-American Studies	Early Christian Studies
American Indian Studies	Earth & Space Science
Anatomy and Cell Biology	East Asian Studies
Animal Sciences	Ecology and Evolutionary Biology
Dance/Movement Therapy	Ecopsychology

Engineering

Economics

English

Education

Germanic Languages

Germanic Languages

Greek

Health Services

Hispanic Languages & Literature

Historic Preservation

History

History and Philosophy of Science

Human Genetics

Human Resource Management

Indo-European Studies

Indo-Tibetan Buddhism

Information Studies

International Cultural Studies

International Management

Islamic Studies

Italian

Jack Kerouac School of Disembodied Poetics

Kinesiology and Leisure Science

Korean

Korean Studies

Japanese

Japanese Studies

Latin

Linguistics Library & Information Services

Literature

Marine Biology

Master of Divinity

Master of Publishing Health for Health Professionals

Mathematics

Mechanical Engineering

Medicine

Medieval Studies

Meteorology

Microbiology, Immunology, & Molecular Genetics

Molecular Biology

Molecular, Cell, & Developmental Biology

Molecular, Cellular, & Integrative Physiology

Molecular & Medical Pharmacology

Molecular Toxicology

Moving Image Archive Studies

Museum Studies

Music

Musicology

Natural Resources and Environmental Management

Neuroscience

Nursing

Nutrition

Ocean and Resources Engineering

Ocean Policy

Oceanography

Pacific Islands Studies

Philippine Studies

Philosophy

Physics

Physiology

Political Science

Population Studies

Portuguese

Psychology

Public Affairs

Romance Languages and Literatures

Religious Studies

Second Language Acquisition

Second Language Studies

Social Welfare

Social Work

Sociology

Somatic Counseling

Spanish

Spanish & Portuguese Studies

Special Education

Speech

Theater

Theater: Contemporary
Performance

Theology

Transpersonal Psychology

Travel Industry Management

Tropical Medicine

Tropical Plant and Soil Sciences

Tropical Plant Pathology

Urban and Regional Management

Wilderness Therapy Women's
Studies

Writing and Poetics

Zoology

> **Tip #8: If your degree is aimed at increasing your income,
> select the program that aligns most with your current
> professional field. If you wish to earn a graduate degree for
> personal enhancement reasons, select the program which most
> interests you, but which you also believe you can complete.**

If you are pursuing a graduate degree to earn more money, you would be best advised to pursue a degree that most aligns with your professional field. Those who work in the business sector may wish to pursue a master's in business administration (MBA®), in which case you will need to take the Graduate Management Admission Test (GMAT®), not the GRE. Teachers of middle and high schools will want to pursue a degree in Education or in their teaching field of expertise. Historians or museum curators would select graduate degrees appropriate to their field of study, as would clinical psychologists.

Pursuing a graduate degree for personal enhancement reasons can be rewarding and lead to unexpected personal and business opportunities.

Again, as discussed in Chapter 1, it is far more common for someone to pursue a Master's degree for non-academic or non-scholastic reasons than it is for someone to pursue a Ph.D. for these reasons. Nonetheless, if you do decide to pursue either a Master's degree or Ph.D. for personal enhancement reasons or to simply earn more money in your field, you will need to take the GRE and go through the entire admissions process. You should select a program which most interests you and be prepared to give the admissions committee extremely compelling reasons for why you should earn a seat in their program.

> **Tip #9: Look at the degree program
> requirements for a few different schools.**

Do they require the GRE? Does their Web site emphasize any particular portions of the GRE in its admission process? For example, one who wishes to procure a graduate degree in philosophy from the University of California-Los Angeles (UCLA) must pursue a Ph.D. degree. Candidates may earn the MA degree while completing the Ph.D. requirements, but must ultimately pursue the Ph.D. The philosophy department at UCLA requires candidates to submit GRE scores that conform to the university's standards, which are not posted on the program's Web site. A UCLA philosophy graduate degree candidate would have to contact the graduate admissions office at UCLA to find out the GRE score requirements for graduate admissions.

Conversely, if one wished to obtain a graduate degree in philosophy from the University of South Florida (USF), one would quickly find that the program itself has GRE scoring requirements for admissions, which exceed the university's general requirements. The USF graduate school posts a minimum score of 1000 (verbal + quantitative). The philosophy department, though, cites "competitive scores" as at least a 600 in verbal, 600 in quantitative (minimum score of 1200), and a minimum analytical writing score of 5.0. If one wished to apply to USF's English department for a Master's degree, one would need to produce a GRE verbal score of 600. The English department cites that it does not determine the quantitative score as a determining factor in admissions. Moreover, this department's analytical writing score requirement is a 4.0. USF's English department requires a GRE verbal reasoning score of 650 for the Ph.D. program.

Another example: One who wishes to apply for a graduate degree in English at Notre Dame University will find that the school does not even post a minimum GRE score requirement, as they state that the GRE test is only one part of the criteria utilized for the admissions process.

You should spend at least a week or two exploring programs at various universities. You may find that the program in which you desire to take courses is only offered at a school that does not even require the GRE or does not require a minimum GRE score. Conversely, you may find that you wish to enter a program which will focus its admission requirements more on the verbal section than the math, or vice versa. You will then focus your studies accordingly.

Tip #10: Talk to one of your professors from your undergraduate years.

If you have been in school recently, this should be easy. Alternatively, you could use the phone book or Internet to look up a department and then speak to one of their faculty or staff. When it comes to deciding what graduate program you will enter—whether for a Master's degree or Ph.D. — there is no reason to reinvent the wheel. If you wish to pursue an academic career, talk to some of your previous professors and get some advice. What program do they recommend you enter? How do they recommend you focus your GRE studies? If you wish to procure a graduate degree to increase your earnings in your current professional field, you may wish to speak to someone at the company for which you already work. If you are a teacher, you can likely access pay salary scales online to complete a comparison analysis of bachelor's to Master's degree earning differences. If you work for a company that may offer you additional promotional opportunities if you have a graduate degree, you may wish to sit down with someone in the company and discuss your future in the field. If you are pursuing a graduate degree for personal enhancement reasons, I thoroughly recommend that you talk to several people about this. Talk to professors, people at your job, your family, friends, and anyone else you know. See if you can find people who pursued graduate degrees that they have used in unexpected and unique ways. This may provide you with additional guidance and inspiration.

CHAPTER 2 HOMEWORK

1. Solidify your reason for pursuing a graduate degree. Again, here are the

possible reasons:

- You want to become a college or university teacher/professor

- You want to earn more money in your current field/profession

- You want to receive personal enhancement

- You do not want to grow up and face the real world of bills and responsibilities customary of what we call "life"

As part of your admissions process, you will most likely need to write an essay on your career goals and why you wish to enter the program to which you are making an application. So, write a one-page essay on why you want to pursue a graduate degree. Type, edit, and proofread your essay, just exactly as if you plan to turn it into an admissions committee.

2. Conduct research on graduate programs offered at various schools throughout the country. You can refer to the list in this chapter for ideas and inspiration. and **www.gradschools.com** is also a good resource for exploring various graduate programs. Write down your top three choices of graduate programs.

3. Choose the graduate program that you wish to enter.

◆ CHAPTER 3

Deciding Which School You Wish to Attend

Deciding which school you wish to attend for graduate studies is one of the most important decisions you will make in this process. It is a critical decision for several reasons: (1) Graduate school requires a significant investment of time and energy; you should spend your time at a school you truly want to attend; (2) Different schools may have varying requirements for the GRE portion of the admissions process; (3) Some schools may offer attractive scholarships, fellowships, and graduate assistantship positions to assist you in financing your graduate education.

Choosing a school should not be taken lightly. Now that you have clearly defined your reason for pursuing a graduate degree, and have also selected the graduate program you wish to enter, selecting the schools you wish to send your application materials to should not be too overbearing.

Tip #11: Determine if you qualify for scholarships.

You may qualify for scholarships and fellowships. Now that you have selected the graduate program you wish to enter, you can choose a few universities to which you wish to apply and visit their department's Web site. For example, if you have decided that you want to pursue a degree in geology, you could go to the Geology Department Web site at any school throughout the entire country. On that Web site, you will find a plethora of information, including admissions criteria, and also scholarship, fellowship, and graduate assistantship information. You can also check the financial aid Web sites at each of the schools you wish to consider. Check out the list of available scholarships. Do you qualify for any of them? Are there certain GRE scoring requirements for any of the scholarships? If so, you will want to remember this during your GRE preparation process. Always aim higher than the required scores.

> **Tip #12: Decide if you plan to finance your own education or if you intend to take out federal and/or private loans.**

If you do not plan on pursuing a scholarship, fellowship, or graduate assistantship, you are most likely planning on financing your own graduate education, either through private loans, public loans, or a combination of both. Conversely, you may have the finances available to fund your own education. If you choose to pay for your own schooling, there will be no minimum GRE requirement as there would be if you applied for a scholarship, so it is important to determine your financing choice early on.

> **Tip #13: Make a list of at least five to ten schools that you wish to attend.**

Based on why you want a degree, what program you wish to pursue, and your research on financial assistantships, begin to narrow down a list of five to ten schools that you wish to send your application materials to. Take time to do your research. You may wonder why you should list five to ten universities. Unless you have an impeccable academic and community service record and can write an admissions essay that will undoubtedly knock the socks off of the admissions committee, you should be aware that you may not get accepted to all the schools to which you send your application. If you make a list of at least three to five schools and get accepted into all of them, you will have several options at your disposal when it comes time to decide which school you will attend. Conversely, if you apply to five schools and only two accept you, you will continue to have options. On the flip side, if you only apply to one school and do not get accepted, you will have lost valuable time and will possibly need to wait one semester to a year before sending out your application materials again. You also should keep in mind the competitiveness of graduate and doctorate degree programs. Even with an impeccable test score, your application could be rejected because of an extremely competitive admissions process. Keeping all these factors in mind should motivate you to strive for the highest test scores and an excellent application profile to submit to multiple schools so you stand the best chance of being accepted.

Tip #14: Once you have the list of schools you intend to apply to, learn about their general graduate admissions requirements.

Now that you know what program you wish to apply to and have made a list of the schools to which you will send your application materials, go to their graduate admissions Web sites and check their general graduate admissions requirements, including GPA and GRE scores. You should know that you must meet at least the minimum university GRE scoring requirements for graduate admissions. Keep a file with this information or take notes.

Tip #15: If necessary, go to the program's Web site for each of the schools you plan to attend and find out what the GRE requirements are.

Do you remember the example from the last chapter? While university Y may require a 1000 minimum score on the GRE general test, university Y's philosophy department (the program you may wish to apply to) may require a 1200 on the GRE general test. Moreover, university Y may not have any requirement posted for the analytical writing section score on the GRE general test. Yet university Y's philosophy department may require a minimum score of a 4.0. Start taking notes and keep all your notes in one place. You must gather this data to strategize your study plan for the GRE.

CHAPTER 3 HOMEWORK

1. Decide how you plan to finance your graduate education. Here are some of the options:

    • Pay for it out of pocket

    • Get federal student loans

    • Secure private loans

    • Procure a combination of federal and private loans

    • Apply for scholarships

    • Apply for fellowships

    • Apply for a position as a graduate assistant (GA), which will help fund the majority of your graduate education

So, what is your plan?

2. Make a list of five to ten schools to which you would like to apply for graduate program admissions.

3. Visit the graduate admissions, financial aid, and individual program Web sites at each of the schools on your list. If you are planning to apply for a scholarship, fellowship, and/or a graduate assistantship, make note of any special GRE scoring requirements. You may also wish to contact someone at the individual departments at each school and inquire as to whether a higher GRE score would increase your chances of securing a scholarship, fellowship, or graduate assistantship.

4. Start a file or notebook to keep track of all this information. Label it "Graduate School Applications." Do not store this on your computer. If you do research on the computer, print out appropriate pages and keep them all in your notebook. This will help keep you organized throughout the graduate admissions application process.

CHAPTER 4

How Attending Graduate School Will Change Your Life

Now that you have decided which school and program you wish to enter, you need to prepare yourself for how graduate school will change your life. You might wonder, at this point, what this has to do with scoring higher on the GRE. But to most efficiently prepare for the GRE, you must be fully committed to the process. The clearer you are about why you want a degree, which degree you want, what school you want to go to, what their program requirements are, and how graduate school will change your life, the more you will begin to emphasize in your mind how critical the GRE is, and subsequently, how important it is that you take your GRE preparations as seriously as possible. For those individuals who already know exactly what school you want to attend, precisely which program you wish to enter, and feel 99 percent confident that you will gain admission — and want nothing more in life at the moment — you could possibly skip this chapter. All others would be well served to spend at least a brief time considering the enormous commitment that graduate school requires.

Tip #16: Decide whether you will attend part- or full-time.

If you are serious about attending graduate school, do you plan on attending full- or part-time? Double check any scholarships that you plan to apply for, as most of them require full-time enrollment. Also, many graduate assistants are required to teach three to four courses and take a minimum of four courses (12 credit hours) per semester. Are you sure that you are prepared for this major life change?

Tip #17: Decide if you will work full- or part-time during your graduate education.

If you are going to attend graduate school part-time, you will likely be able to decide whether you wish to work full- or part-time around your school schedule. If you plan to attend graduate school full-time, you may only be able to work part-time, if at all. If you plan on procuring a graduate assistantship position, you will almost certainly not have time for any other work outside your GA duties and the classes you will take. Your pay for being a GA will not likely be substantial, so it is important to decide if this is the right decision for you.

Tip #18: Talk to any friends and family who have been to graduate school.

Talk to anybody and everybody you know who has been to graduate school and completed it. What advice would they give someone starting the admissions process? If they had to do it all over again, would they change anything? Were they able to "have a life" while attending graduate school? If not, will you be alright with that?

CASE STUDY: SANDRA ROMO

California Baptist University
Riverside, California
Sandra.romo@calbaptist.edu

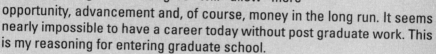

Life as a Graduate Student

Upon graduation with a bachelor's degree there is a little unknown secret for the recent graduates. Obtaining a graduate degree will allow more opportunity, advancement and, of course, money in the long run. It seems nearly impossible to have a career today without post graduate work. This is my reasoning for entering graduate school.

Of course there is the sacrifice made by a lot of work and significant time lost in the life of a graduate student. However, it is nearly impossible to obtain certain career goals without a graduate degree, so the sacrifice is essential.

As I pursue my master's degree as a graduate student, I know that the long weekends and missed events are worth the result of a better career, as well as the education received. In the perspective of things it seems that professors, deans and other university officials give a certain amount of respect to the individuals that come back to school as a graduate. I complete each assignment knowing that I am studying a specialized subject that I chose. Now that I know what I want to do with my life, this will help me tremendously.

It seems that a common misconception of undergraduate students is that they have not yet entered a career and simply 'think' they know what they want to do with their lives. It is not until after graduation and obtaining a less than satisfying job that there is a realization that a graduate degree will help.

I chose to pursue my graduate degree to help my family and myself. My husband and I both know that there will be sacrifices because of the work. However, in the end, we feel the sacrifice is worth the outcome. I would tell anyone considering a graduate degree to pursue it. This venture of hard work, long nights and missed weekends is worth the outcome: a better career and education.

Tip #19: Consider how graduate school will affect your relationships.

Going to graduate school will undoubtedly affect your relationships. You will probably have less time to spend with your family and friends. If you are married or have a significant other, you will not be able to have as much private time for dates and other events. When I went through my master's degree program, I spent most of my evenings and weekends writing papers and studying for tests while my husband kicked back, watched TV, or went out and had fun. If this was your upcoming situation, would you have a problem with that? Are you truly prepared to make this sacrifice? If not, you may wish to reconsider graduate school, and subsequently the GRE. If you are not prepared to make the necessary sacrifices that graduate school requires, you can always apply and go later. If you feel unsure about this and proceed anyway, you will experience complications in your attempts to score higher on the GRE.

Tip #20: Consider the impact graduate school will have on your social life.

When I went to graduate school for my master's degree, I missed most family events. I frequently had to write a paper, do research, or work on something school-related. I also rarely enjoyed the opportunity of just having dinner or coffee with a friend. You should not underestimate the impact that going to graduate school will have on your social life. Make sure that you are ready for this change, especially if you plan to move out of state for your graduate education.

Conversely, you will make friends at school in your program. If you plan to live in a dorm, you may also make friends there. Additionally, you can get involved with clubs and activities on campus. It is not that you will not have a life, it will just be an entirely different one. If you are alright with this, then your commitment to the graduate admissions process (which includes the GRE) should be renewed by now. If this does not feel right to you, please take the time to reconsider.

> **Tip #21: Consider how graduate school will further or hinder your career.**

Are you currently working full-time somewhere? Will you need to abandon your current job to procure a graduate education? Is this acceptable to you? Conversely, will getting your graduate degree further your career and possibly help you earn more money? Consider both sides of the coin.

> **Tip #22: Consider the time sacrifice involved in graduate school.**

Whether you attend full- or part-time, the time sacrifice required will be tremendous. Do not underestimate this, as graduate education will consume your life. Make sure you are prepared for this. You will most likely live on campus—figuratively speaking.

> **Tip #23: Consider the financial investment of graduate school.**

Remember: Loans do have to be paid back. When I graduated with my master's degree, I had $25,000 in student loans. That is a significant amount of money to owe anyone. Each dime must be paid back.

If you plan to procure scholarships, fellowships, and or a GA position, this will help. Remember, though, that you will probably not be able to work any other jobs while taking courses and teaching at the university. You will therefore miss out on years which you could have earned a full-time income and put money into your retirement account. Is this still what you want?

Tip #24: Decide whether graduate school is truly for you.

If you feel certain about your purpose for getting a graduate degree, know to what program you want to apply, be certain about which schools you wish to attend, and feel confident that you can make the time, social, and financial sacrifices necessary to procure your graduate degree. You sound like you have your feet on solid ground and are ready to rock and roll. If, though, any of these aspects are unclear to you, you should stop for a few weeks to reconsider. You may wish to talk to some of your old professors to get advice. Talk to people who have been to graduate school and see what they say. You may even wish to seek the assistance of a psychologist. Graduate school is fun but serious business. So is preparing for the GRE. Do not embark on this journey until you are truly ready.

Tip #25: If you plan to proceed with your graduate school plans, write an affirmation and read it out loud every day.

Affirmations are normally written in the present tense. When read daily, they affirm your commitment to a given project or attitude. If you plan to proceed with your GRE preparation and graduate school admissions process, write an affirmation which you can read daily to support your efforts. Here is an example:

"I am grateful for scoring a 600 on the verbal section of the GRE and gaining admissions into the Master's degree in English program at the University of South Florida."

Here is another example:

"I am grateful for scoring as high a score as possible on the general GRE test, so that I can have the greatest chance of receiving a scholarship at Notre Dame University."

Affirmations do work, when reading with purposeful intention.

At this point, it is time for you to rock and roll—or not. If you are still in, buckle up, roll up your sleeves, and get ready to work.

If you have changed your mind about graduate school or feel that you need more time to consider this decision, congratulations on following your heart and listening to your head. You just may well save yourself considerable time, effort, money, and valuable relationships in the process.

CHAPTER 4 HOMEWORK

1. Make a list of the sacrifices that will be required of you to enter graduate school.

2. Spend at least three days considering whether you truly wish to make these sacrifices right now in your life.

3. If you have decided to proceed with your GRE preparations and graduate school admissions process, write your affirmation on a piece of paper and put it somewhere that you will see and read it daily. Then, start reading it every day.

Preparing to Take the GRE

If you are on the fence about whether you want to go to graduate school, that is alright. Be warned, though, you are about to invest a considerable amount of time and money in your ambiguous uncertainty. Developing and following a study schedule will take time and effort. Registering for the GRE will cost money. If you are on the fence about whether you want to do this, please be sure that you wish to proceed.

While it is not ideal to be on the fence, it is not entirely unheard of, either. Some of the anxiety or uncertainty that you are feeling may simply be a reflection of the uneasiness you feel about starting something as significant as graduate school. Try to relax and take it easy with yourself. Be honest with yourself at all times. Follow your heart and you will never go wrong. A word of comfort: If you are reading this book, you want to take the GRE and go to graduate school. You would have stopped reading this book by now and be headed for the beach if this was absolutely not meant for you. Be careful though. Be honest with yourself at all times, for your own benefit. Are you feeling pressure from family or friends? Do you feel like you might let people down if you do not go through with this? These are not valid reasons to continue and expend your own time, money and valuable energy. Conversely, it is possible that you do want to do this and may perceive interest that you receive from family and friends as "pressure." Only you know the difference. I remember how much anxiety I felt about both the test and entering graduate school. Unfortunately, I used to have low self-esteem. Subconsciously, even though I did not realize it, I did not think I deserved to score well on the GRE or go to graduate school. Ultimately, I just had to follow my heart and keep going. I had a burning desire inside that kept ablaze. Do you feel that desire? That is how you know this is for you.

Regardless of what you decide, it is now time to proceed in the more technical aspects of preparing for your GRE. Remember: this is your life and your race or marathon, so you decide. If you have decided to continue the process — congratulations. Now, take a look at the GRE general test registration process and also address how you will develop a study process.

Tip #26: Determine the application deadline for the departments of the five to ten schools to which you plan to apply.

It is essential that you know the deadlines for the programs to which you wish to apply. Also, you must make certain to distinguish between master's and doctoral level program deadlines, as they may differ. If you do not do this homework ahead of time, your GRE studies may be seriously derailed altogether.

You may wonder what graduate program deadlines have to do with scoring higher on the GRE. While some schools accept applications year-round and have a wide range of application deadlines, many universities only accept applications one time per year. If, for example, you wish to apply to the master's program at a university which only accepts applications in the fall, and the fall entrance admission application date has just passed, you may wish to wait several months before you actually take your GRE. This will give you more time to study. One possible negative: You will need to wait longer than you expected to begin attending the number one university of your choice. You may also ultimately decide that you do not want to wait that long to commence your graduate studies and decide not to send your application to that university.

Follow these instructions to determine the application deadlines for the departments of the five to ten schools to which you play to apply. Be certain to write the deadlines down on a piece of paper. Post the paper in a location that is visible to you every day. Alternatively, begin a file and label it "GRE test." Place the application deadlines in the file.

1. Take out your list of the five to ten schools you plan to apply to.

2. Look up and write down the Web sites for each of those schools.

3. Go to the Web site for the first school choice on your list to which you plan to apply.

4. Find the section for "Graduate Studies." Check this section first to see if there are any general deadlines for the school as a whole.

5. Locate the program Web site for the school. For example, if you plan to apply for a Ph.D. in philosophy from the University of Miami, find the links or go to the Web site for the Department of Philosophy at the University of Miami.

6. Locate the link for "graduate studies." The link may not contain this precise wording. Essentially, you need to find the section of the department's Web site that gives information about application deadlines for both master's and Ph.D. level studies (depending on which level to which you plan to apply).

7. Be sure to check this section carefully for any information about what semesters the program accepts applications. Again, some programs will accept applications every semester, while other programs will only admit students during one particular semester each year.

8. Locate the application deadline for the level of study appropriate to your application. Make sure that if you are applying for a Master's degree, that you get the master's degree application deadline. The Ph.D. application deadline may differ.

9. Locate the phone number to the department from the Web site.

10. Call the department to verify that the application deadline listed on the Web site is correct.

11. Repeat these steps for each of the schools you plan to apply to.

12. Ultimately, you will have a list of five to ten application deadlines.

Tip #27: Determine how much time stands between you and the application deadline for the semester you wish to enter graduate school in a particular school's program.

Now that you have determined the application deadlines for the programs to which you plan to apply, you can now evaluate how much time stands between you and the application deadlines. This step is critical and should not be overlooked. For example, if you cannot apply to the program of your choice for another full year, you will not want to register to take the GRE for at least another six to seven months. Alternatively, you may discover that the deadline to apply to the program you wish to enter will come to pass within the next month. You must then begin to make a critical decision about what semester you can truly enter the program of your choice.

Tip #28: Determine whether you can enter the program during the semester you wish to or not.

For example, if you want to apply to the Ph.D. program in English Literature at the University of Florida and you discover that they only admit students in the fall and that the deadline for fall applications will pass within two weeks, you will have to decide whether you are willing to wait an entire year to enter that program or not. If you discover that an application deadline is approaching within two to three weeks, this is simply not enough time to properly prepare for the GRE, let alone secure all the application materials—such as transcripts and letters of recommendation—that you will need for your application packet. You will likely need to plan on entering that program the following semester or year.

It is ideal to allow yourself three to four months for the graduate program application process. This gives you a sufficient amount of time to prepare for the GRE, to allow yourself the opportunity to schedule a retake of your GRE if necessary (in the event that you do not obtain the scores you desire) and to procure other necessary documents, such as transcripts and letters of recommendation. You do not want to send in an incomplete application package.

Tip #29: Adjust your semester entrance date, if necessary.

Now that you have determined the application deadlines for the programs you wish to enter at your desired schools, you must now decide what semester you can realistically enter the program. Again, it is ideal to allow three to four months for the graduate application process. Think optimistically. Assume that with three to four months of preparation time and leeway, you will obtain the desired scores you wish to achieve on the GRE and will procure all of the necessary documentation for your application.

Make adjustments as necessary. If the next deadline for the program you wish to enter is in one month, plan on commencing studies in that program the following semester instead. The semester that you have to wait will not be wasted; you will use that time to properly prepare for the GRE.

Take out your piece of paper with all your graduate program application deadlines. Make adjustments as necessary. Cross out deadlines and replace with new, appropriate deadlines according to the research you do and decisions you make.

**Tip #30: According to the deadlines you
are working with, register to take the GRE.**

Base your GRE test date on the application deadlines for the top three schools to which you wish to send your graduate school application.

Although this may at first appear as a quagmire or conundrum, careful thought and preparation can guide you through this process.

This way, if you do well on the exam, you are automatically covered for all of the application deadlines for all of your top schools. If you do not perform as well as you would have liked, you have plenty of time to re-test for your top school, as well as your other choices of schools.

You can retake the GRE once a month, every 30 days. You may take it up to a maximum of five times per calendar year.

**Tip #31: Determine the dates that
you will re-test for the GRE, if necessary.**

Understandably, many students may feel challenged to plan dates on which they will retake the GRE, when they have not even taken their first GRE yet. Some students may view this as planning for failure. Others may feel completely confident that they will perform and score well, and feel that they will not possibly need to take the test a second or even third time.

Planning the dates on which you can retake the GRE does not mean that you are planning for failure. This does not mean that you will not study just as hard, because you would not necessarily want to take the test twice. Your decision to allow yourself the breathing room — time wise — to retake the GRE is simply a contingency plan. There are actually several reasons that you may need to retake the GRE:

- You may not score as well as you would have liked to because unexpected circumstances arose in your life which prevented you from following your study schedule as closely as you would have liked.

- You may experience unanticipated anxiety on test day and therefore not perform as well as you would have preferred.

- Unexpected circumstances of a dramatic nature may occur between your GRE registration date and the date of the test itself. You may become seriously ill. A family member may become seriously ill.

- You may find yourself under the weather on test day and therefore not able to perform as well as you had expected.

- Something unanticipated may occur on the test day that prevents you from even reaching the testing center. For example, you get a flat tire and cannot find anyone to give you a ride, or you oversleep and miss your test.

While these possible scenarios are not meant to scare you or make you think of all of the negative circumstances that could arise, they are intended to make you think about life realistically. The good news is that you can think carefully about all of these scenarios and do the best you can to prepare for any unexpected possibilities, while also releasing what you cannot control. You are planning dates to retake your GRE to simply give yourself peace of mind. You can study hard and rest easy at night, knowing that if something happens which prevents you from performing successfully on your actual GRE test date, you have backup plans in place that will assist you. You will be able to get into the school of your choice because you were smart and mature enough to think and plan ahead. This peace of mind will help you score higher on the GRE.

Tip #32: Procure a file folder and label it "GRE Test."

It is essential that you begin organizing yourself for the graduate school application process. If you have not already done so, now is the time to procure a folder and label it "GRE Test."

I recommend that you buy a notebook for any note taking and also start a "folder" on your computer.

Tip #33: Put your GRE registration information into that folder, along with any information you have collected about various schools and programs.

You should put any and all information related to the GRE in this folder, including any Web site information from various graduate school and program Web sites. You should also include your list of the top five to ten schools and the deadlines for the various programs to which you wish to send your application.

Keep this file handy. That way, whenever you have a question about your GRE or your graduate school application process, you can quickly access the folder and obtain the information you need.

Tip #34: Put your GRE test date on your calendar.

If you do not already have a calendar or planner, you must go buy one. It is essential that you put your GRE test date on your calendar. This may seem obvious, but believe it or not, you may find yourself so caught up in all of the preparation details, such as researching schools and programs, writing down deadline dates and studying, that you completely forget to mark it on your calendar.

Not only should you mark your GRE test date on your calendar, you should also post it somewhere visible where you can see it every day, like your refrigerator or bathroom mirror. This concept is not meant to irritate you or cause you anxiety. Rather, seeing your test date every day will keep it in front of your face in the unlikely event that you become remiss in following your study schedule. You are embarking on a serious study and preparation process. You are going to live and breathe the GRE for the next several months or weeks.

Tip #35: According to the time that you have to prepare for the GRE, create a study schedule for yourself.

For example, determine that you will study on Mondays, Wednesdays, and Fridays from 7 p.m. to 9 p.m. Or, determine that you will study every Saturday and Sunday from 12 p.m. to 4 p.m. These are just examples. Decide how many hours you want to put into your study time each week. Then, schedule that time on your personal calendar, just like you would any other appointment. It is also preferable for you to type out your schedule for at least a month in advance and post it somewhere that you can see it regularly.

This step is critical. While your brains and talent will help you on your GRE, so will basic organization skills. It is essential that you assign the same value to your GRE study time as you do anything else. You must make a study schedule and put your study times on your calendar, just as you would put a date, concert or anything else important. If you do not decide ahead of time what days and times you will study for the GRE, there is a reasonably high chance that you will just not study. This does not mean that you are an inherently lazy person, this is simply human nature.

For example, as I write this book, I follow my own writing plan or schedule. When I first decided to write this book, I did not just say to myself, "OK, some day I am going to write a book about how to score higher on the GRE." I developed a specific timetable as to how, when and where I would complete the book. I determined which days and nights of the week I would write the book. I then chose which time periods during those days and nights I would write. I also worked out how many words I would write on which days. I then put these writing "appointment" times on my calendar, just like I did everything else in my life, like social activities and other obligations. Had I not taken this approach, I might have just left the writing of this book to fate or chance. Had I left the production of this book to my mood or daily whim, you might not be reading this book right now.

Developing a study plan is not difficult. You must first make a commitment to yourself to study. You must accept:

- That *you* must choose the number of hours you wish to study for the GRE each week.

- That *you* must schedule those hours amidst other activities during the week.

- That completing these first two tasks implicates *sacrifice*. For example, if you wish to study at least 15 hours per week for your GRE, and you only have 20 extra hours per week right now, after classes and other social and/or family obligations. You must accept the fact that you are only going to have five hours of free time each week.

Sacrifice is indeed a key word here. But remember that the sacrifice is temporary and the fruits of your labor represent your seedling dream in the acorn of your deepest desires: graduate school.

Below is an example of a study plan. You can review this and then turn to the notes and homework section of this chapter to develop your own. Keep in mind that you will want to consider your own life and schedule when developing your study plan. If you are an adult who graduated ten years ago and works a full-time job Monday-Friday, you may decide that you want to complete most of your studying on the weekends. If, though, you are currently a student and work on Saturdays and Sundays and have Tuesdays and Wednesdays off, you may wish to do a good portion of your studying on Tuesdays and Wednesdays. Conversely, many people may want to do all of their studying during Monday through Friday so that they can have Saturdays and Sundays off from studying, regardless of whether they work those days. The beauty of developing your *own* study plan is just that: It is your *own*.

CHAPTER 5 HOMEWORK

1. Determine the application deadlines for the schools and programs to which you wish to apply. Again, write down or type these on a piece of paper. Put this piece of paper in a file and label it "GRE Test."

2. Based on how much time you want to study and other factors discussed in this chapter, determine which semester you can realistically enter the program(s) of your choice.

3. Register for the GRE at the following Web site: **www.ets.org.**

4. Determine dates on which you can retest for the GRE, if necessary.

5. Put your GRE test date on your calendar or planner. If you do not currently own a calendar or planner, go out and buy one now.

6. Choose the date that you will start studying for the GRE.

7. Decide how many hours per week you plan to commit to your GRE studies.

8. Develop your own study plan. You can use this template as a guide.

SAMPLE GRE STUDY PLAN

Commitment: 15 hours per week (Six for verbal reasoning; six for quantitative reasoning; three for analytical writing)

Sundays:	Two hours verbal, one hour analytical writing
Mondays:	Two hours quantitative
Tuesdays:	Two hours quantitative, one hour analytical writing
Wednesdays:	OFF
Thursdays:	Two hours verbal, one hour analytical writing
Fridays:	OFF
Saturdays:	Two hours verbal, two hours quantitative

SAMPLE GRE STUDY PLAN
Commitment: ___ hours per week (___ for verbal reasoning; ___ for quantitative reasoning; ___ for analytical writing)
Sundays:
Mondays:
Tuesdays:
Wednesdays:
Thursdays:
Fridays:
Saturday:

9. Put your study dates on your calendar, just as you would any other social activity, class or obligation.

10. Post your GRE test date somewhere visible, like on your refrigerator or bathroom mirror.

CHAPTER 6

Making Necessary Social Announcements and Adjustments to Embark on <u>Your GRE Preparation Process</u>

By now, you should have already:

- Decided why you want to get a graduate degree

- Made a firm commitment to the GRE study process as well as entering graduate school

- Developed an affirmation that you cite on a regular basis to assist you with your goals in this arena

- Decided what school you want to attend

- Decided what program you wish to enter

- Determined the application deadlines for the programs and schools to which you intend to send your application

- Considered the program deadlines and decided what semester you can realistically enter the top school(s) of your choice

- Selected the date on which you must first take the GRE

- Registered for the GRE

- Started a "GRE" folder

- Placed all of your research on schools, departments, programs and your GRE test date in your GRE folder

- Put your GRE test date on your calendar

- Placed your GRE test date somewhere visible that you can see it every day (e.g. your refrigerator or the bathroom mirror)

- Developed a study plan that encompasses all of the time between now and the date that you plan to take the GRE

- Made a commitment to your study plan

It is now time to briefly address how all of this will inevitably affect your social life. Do not underestimate the GRE. It is not realistic for you to maintain the same social life while preparing for the GRE. As rough as this might sound, it is actually a good thing. When you get to graduate school and find yourself fully immersed in your graduate studies, you will be forced to face the unavoidable impact on your social life.

> **Tip #36: If you are married or have a boyfriend or girlfriend, make sure that this person is aware of the study schedule you created in Chapter 5.**

By now, you should have already discussed your graduate school plans with your partner, significant other or spouse. I hope he or she supports you in your endeavors.

Speaking from personal experience, I know that many spouses simply do not understand the commitment involved in preparing for the GRE or in going to graduate school, unless they have previously embarked on that journey. You do not want to surprise your significant other and suddenly become unavailable for dates, goof-off days, and so on. You should extend the courtesy of an advanced notice to them.

Make an appointment with your significant other to discuss your study schedule plan. If he or she supports your plans to attend graduate school, he or she will support your study plan. Let your partner or spouse know how important he or she is to you. Make sure to tell them that the extra time you are about to begin devoting to your GRE studies does not mean that you do not care about them. Sit down together and try to come up with creative solutions that address how you can follow your study plan, fulfill your other obligations and also spend time with your partner or significant other.

It might also be helpful to post your study schedule on the refrigerator. If your spouse knows that you plan to study for the GRE every Tuesday night from 7 p.m. to 9 p.m., he or she may wish to make his or her own standing commitment for that evening. If you communicate with your partner ahead of time, you offer him or her the honor and respect he or she deserves in this process.

CASE STUDY/INTERVIEW: KAREN CARD

Certified Relationship Coach
P.O. Box 4887
Clearwater, Florida 33758-4887
727-535-8393
www.CoachingForLove.net

Communicating With Your Spouse

As creatures of habit, we tend to expect certain behaviors from our partners. These expectations may include a certain amount of time spent together each week and a certain amount of positive attention and physical intimacy.

When one partner embarks on a new, time-consuming project, like studying for the GRE, it is natural that the other partner may feel ignored,

CASE STUDY/INTERVIEW: KAREN CARD

unimportant and possibly even resentful. To avoid these negative feelings, good communication is critical.

Talk to your partner ahead of time and warn them of the upcoming changes in your availability. Set new expectations on the amount of time you will be spending together. Reassure them that this extra time apart is only temporary, and that you are missing them as much as they are missing you.

Another important point to maintaining a healthy relationship is that you do not eliminate "date night." While you may be tempted to change your current "date night" into "study night," do not do this. Your partner deserves your uninterrupted, focused attention and personal conversation at least once a month, but preferably once a week. Plan to continue a regular "date night" no matter what. Besides keeping your relationship healthy, your brain needs a night off occasionally, too.

Keeping these ideas in mind will allow you to maintain a healthy relationship with your partner while you are transitioning into your new, busier schedule. Remember, good communication is the key to any successful relationship.

Tip #37: Announce to family members that you will be studying for the GRE and may not be as available for social gatherings and family functions.

Give your family the same courtesy that you give your partner, spouse or significant other, particularly if you have a close-knit family that gets together on a frequent basis.

By now, if your family does not already know about your plans to attend graduate school, you should tell them. You should also advise them about your upcoming GRE test date. Give them your test date, gently remind them that you may not have as much free time as usual, but that you still love and appreciate them.

> **Tip #38: Announce your GRE preparation plans to friends and ask for their support.**

You should also tell your friends about your GRE preparation plans. As a previous GRE test taker, I do recommend studying at least 10 to 20 hours per week for the GRE over a period of two to three months. This will curb your social life. Let your friends know in advance about your plans to attend graduate school. Tell them that you plan to prepare for the GRE exam over the course of the upcoming months and ask for their support.

> **Tip #39: Decide whether you want to take a prep course.**

Prep courses can be investigated through the yellow pages, online, or community college and university bulletin board postings. Many reputable and effective prep courses are available for the quantitative reasoning section, verbal reasoning section, or the entire test. You can research where prep courses are offered either online, through the yellow pages, or at your local colleges and universities.

Taking a prep course can certainly help raise your GRE score, although it is not entirely necessary in order to score higher on the GRE. It may even just give you a boost of confidence. In other words, by taking a prep course you may feel that you have truly done all that you can do to prepare for the GRE. Ultimately, you have to make your own choice. Students prepare in different ways.

> **Tip #40: Choose an anxiety reduction technique now, so that you can begin practicing it nearly every day before test time.**

Choosing an anxiety reduction technique and embedding it into the social aspect of your daily life will provide you with valuable assistance on test day. There are several anxiety reducing techniques that you can utilize, such as breath work, positive affirmations, meditation, relaxation, sound therapy and more.

Some of you may already utilize one of these practices. If so, make sure that you schedule regular practice times for your anxiety reducing technique. If you have been somewhat remiss in your meditation or affirmation practices, now is the time to get back on track.

If you have never practiced breath work, affirmations, meditation, relaxation, or anything similar before, this could be an exciting opportunity for you, either in the short-term for test day or the long-term for your entire life.

I have found that a combination of anxiety-reducing tactics help me get through particularly stressful situations. Even though I have already taken the GRE and am in a Ph.D. program, there will always be stressful situations that I will have to face: writing my doctoral dissertation, defending it, or interviewing for future jobs. I have had the most success with breath work, affirmations, meditation, and the emotional freedom technique, or EFT. This technique is an effective form of meridian energy therapy that comprises finger-tapping on various pressure points of the body. Many other people that teach and utilize these techniques, which is why they are included in this book. Feel free to "try on" any one of these techniques and see how they fit and feel.

Whatever you do, choose at least one anxiety reducing technique which you can practice on a regular basis up to and including test day, even if it is simply lying down for ten minutes per day, closing your eyes and relaxing. What you want to do is program your brain to relax around this test, and to complement the cognitive workouts that you are giving it!

CASE STUDY: MELANIE MCGRATH

San Bernardino, California

**Preparing Academically
and Physically for the GRE**

I have never been a successful test taker and I knew that I needed to thoroughly prepare myself for the format of the GRE as well as learn how to manage the physical anxiety that I feel when taking tests. I headed to the local bookstore and bought the Barron GRE test series, which included a computer-based testing preparation disk. Over the course of a six-week period, I devoted an hour per day to studying for the test in both the book and computerized format.

I first took one of the sample tests in the back of the book in order to determine my strengths and weaknesses. The sample tests enabled me to focus my efforts on the analogy, vocabulary, and math sections of the test. I studied the various types of analogies and memorized in detail the vocabulary lists provided. In addition to the Barron test preparation books, I also borrowed high-school math textbooks from the local library in order to review my math skills. Over the six-week period, I continuously monitored my progress on the sample tests and practiced the computer tests twice a week.

Not only did I prepare academically, but I also learned how to manage my anxiety. I visited a local yoga studio and learned breathing techniques, yoga poses, and visualization techniques. During my six-week preparation period, I continued to attend the yoga classes. The anxiety and stress management techniques learned through yoga contributed to a successful score on the GRE.

THE IMPORTANCE OF THE BREATH

Taking a standardized test can be daunting and you may experience many emotions from mild apprehension to outright fear. Practicing breath awareness on a daily basis and learning some simple breathing techniques are sure ways to create more balance in your life. When you improve the quality of your breath, you improve the quality of your life, and, in this case, you are likely to improve your GRE score as well. Make breath awareness part of your study plan. The sooner you begin, the better your results.

Breath training starts with observing the flow of the breath in and out of the body. All you have to do is let yourself follow the air in (inhalation) and follow the flow of air out of the body (exhalation). Practice this every morning before you get out of bed and at various other times throughout the day. After a few days, you can increase your awareness by lying on your stomach and feeling your body rise with the inhalation and fall with the exhalation. This exercise, known as crocodile pose in yoga, releases abdominal tension and facilitates diaphragmatic breathing. You can also turn over and relax on your back to observe the breath. This position, known as corpse pose, is deeply relaxing.

As you continue observing your breath, you will notice irregularities from time to time. These irregularities occur in connection with your thoughts and also in connection with your activities. Learning what kinds of thoughts cause irregularities is an essential step in using the breath to manage your emotions. You may also find the connection between nostril dominance and thoughts and also their combined effects on the body.

If you experience anxiety in a test situation, a breath technique that can help you is to slow the breath. One way to slow the breath is to use a 2 to 1 breath ratio, that is, to make the duration of the exhalation twice as long as the duration of the inhalation. This technique helps to regulate the movement of the lungs and to quiet the nervous system. When you slow the breath, you will slow the nervous agitation in your mind and find it easier to concentrate on the task at hand: your test questions.

For more information on the breath and breath training, consult a trained and certified yoga instructor or read sound yoga texts, such as those published by the Himalayan Yoga Institute Press.

VISUALIZATION

Success is positively linked to creative visualization and you can use visualization to help you improve any area of your life. Including a short visualization period in your GRE study plan can have an amazing effect on your state of mind when you take the exam, and thus on your performance during the exam and your score. You could call this being in the test taking zone.

Pay attention to your thoughts about taking the GRE and getting into the graduate school of your choice. Notice the thoughts which come into your mind most often. Are they constructive and positive thoughts? Do you think about making a good score on the test and entering your graduate program? Are you reading your daily affirmation? Or, do you think about being nervous and worry about taking the test? Your predominant thoughts are the key to your performance in test taking or any other situation in life.

Creative visualization is the conscious creation of an image. It is the inner seeing of an outer result; it is not imagination. Imagination and day dreaming are insubstantial stories that the mind uses for entertainment or escape. They can be interrupted and dissipated by even a slight change in your immediate environment such as the opening of a door or the calling out of your name by a friend or family member. Creative visualization, on the other hand, is the conscious control of your thoughts and perceptions which follow directed plans for success.

To achieve success through creative visualization, you must have faith in yourself and be patient and kind to yourself. Persevere, concentrate, be patient, and use self-discipline. Visualization sharpens your intuition and brings you more in touch with your goals. You become more aware of opportunities as they present themselves, such as the chance to form a GRE study group or the ability to recognize situations such as free lectures and readings that may enhance your broad knowledge base and improve your test scores.

Remez Sasson, a motivational speaker and creator of **www.successconsciousness.com**, has outlined a process to make visualization work for you. The following steps are based on his suggestions and should be practiced every day. (This is the "list" for motivating yourself to succeed).

1. Define your goal.

2. Think, meditate, and listen to your intuition before you start.

3. Sit alone in a quiet place where you will not be disturbed.

4. Relax your body.

5. Take a few deep, rhythmical breaths.

6. Visualize the object or situation that you desire.

7. See a clear, detailed mental image of that object or situation.

8. Use all five physical senses to make the goal real. For example, let yourself mentally experience how it feels to see the score you want to make on the GRE.

9. Put feeling and positive emotion into the experience.

10. Practice at least twice a day for ten minutes at a time.

11. Persevere in these actions until you succeed.

12. When doubts arise, immediately replace them with positive thoughts.

13. Keep your mind open to opportunities.

14. Take advantage of every opportunity that presents itself for your benefit.

MEDITATION

Although meditation is utilized in some parts of the world as a spiritual practice, including the United States, it can also be used as an anxiety reduction technique. Personally, I have practiced meditation since 2005. When I first began a meditation practice, I experienced intense anxiety on a regular basis. I often felt so tense that I had astronomical apprehension. I also experienced panic attacks on a regular basis. Beginning a meditation practice encouraged me to slow down. As I began to practice for 45 minutes each night, I started to get in touch with my body. I realized that I was pushing myself too much and became more sensitive with myself. I also noticed, over time, that my intellectual capacity improved. Moreover, my reactivity to certain "charged" situations — whether stressful tests or unpleasant encounters with various individuals — significantly reduced over time. The practice of meditation can open doors for you. You do not have to make it your spiritual practice, unless that is your desire. Practicing meditation is not difficult and only requires a little time and effort.

CASE STUDY/INTERVIEW: MATTHEW FLICKSTEIN

Meditation Teacher
The Forest Way Insight Meditation Center
Ruckersville, Virginia
www.forestway.org
Meditation Instructions

Calming the Mind

- Your eyes are closed.

- Your mouth is closed and you are breathing through your nose.

- Feel the sensation of your breath as it flows in and out of your nostrils at the tip of your nose. Some people feel the sensation more

CASE STUDY/INTERVIEW: MATTHEW FLICKSTEIN

strongly within the nostrils, while others feel it more on the upper lip.

- To help you locate where you feel the touch sensation of the breath most distinctly, inhale deeply and force the air through your nostrils. Wherever you feel the sensation most clearly and precisely is the place to focus your attention for the balance of the meditation period.

- Feel the beginning, the middle, and the end of every in-breath, and the beginning, the middle, and the end of every out-breath.

- Sometimes the breath will be short — there is no need to make it longer.

- Sometimes the breath will be long — there is no need to make it shorter.

- Sometimes the breath will be erratic — there is no need to even it out.

- Just become aware of the breath as it goes in and out of the nostrils or the tip of the nose.

- Feel the beginning, the middle, and the end of every in-breath and out-breath.

- Let the breath breathe itself.

- Every time your attention moves away from the breath and shifts to a different object of awareness, such as a physical sensation or a thought, gently but firmly draw your attention back to the touch sensation of your breath.

- Continue practicing until the end of the meditation session.

CHAPTER 6 HOMEWORK

1. Talk to your spouse, partner, or significant other about your graduate school and GRE study plans. Consider posting your GRE study schedule on the refrigerator or somewhere visible that your partner can see it.

2. Talk to your friends and family members about your GRE study plans. Explain that your social availability may be curbed somewhat for awhile. Let them know that you love them, and that this time period of intense study is temporary for you.

3. Decide whether you want to take a prep course to help you prepare for the GRE. If so, find out where and when courses are available. Sign up for one if necessary. Build it into your study plan and calendar.

4. Choose an anxiety reducing technique that you would like to begin working with to help calm your nerves. Set aside time each day — if only even for ten minutes — to practice your technique.

CHAPTER 7

The Structure of the GRE

The computer-based GRE has four sections, one of which is experimental and not scored. The analytical writing test is given first and is followed by verbal and quantitative tests and also the unidentified experimental section in the form of an extra verbal or quantitative section. Experimental sections are not scored. There may also be an identified research section as part of the computerized GRE. If such a section is included in your test, it will be the last section given and no scores are given for this section.

Total testing time may be as long as three-and-a-half hours, plus the time it takes to complete the research section if one is included. Please carefully read the directions for each section. The directions will state the total number of questions in the section and the total amount of time allowed for completing the section.

In the computer-based test, just as in the paper test, the analytical writing test is given first. Two issue tasks are presented on screen and you must select the one you wish to address. Only one argument task will be presented for completion.

TEST SCORING

The first question on the computerized GRE will be of medium difficulty. As you answer each question, the computer scores it and uses that information, and the information from preceding questions, along with its programmed information about the test design to select your next questions. This means that two people taking the test on the same day at the same time are not likely to see the same questions in the same order. As long as you answer each question you see correctly, your next question is likely to be more difficult than the previous one. When you answer a question incorrectly, the next question will more often than not be less difficult than the one before.

Because test takers are given questions of varying difficulty on the computer-based test, some people have asked how the computer-based GRE scores can be used to compare the skills of individuals. This is where the test design and standard specifications come into play. The statistical characteristics of each question answered are taken into consideration, thus yielding scores that can be appropriately compared. ETS® has also conducted research which indicated that the scores on the paper test are comparable to the scores earned on the computerized test. Although this type of information may satisfy your curiosity about the two types of tests, your main concern should be how to do well on the GRE. To get a better feeling for how your testing experience and score will be on test day, download the free PowerPrep software from the ETS® Web site that has two GRE CATs for you to practice on. Take the first one under simulated testing conditions to get a fairly accurate experience and score. Note, however, that the real GRE is likely to be harder, so reduce your score on each section by about 60 points to compensate. This practice will give you an approximate indication of how you will do on the test.

TEST MANAGEMENT

If a section of the test, such as a reading passage, is too large to appear in its entirety on the computer screen, you will use the scroll bar to move through the text. The word "beginning" appears on the information line at the top of the screen when you start a question. You can scroll through the material line-by-line or page-by-page depending on how fast you want to go.

You can practice with your tutorial as many times as you need in order to feel comfortable when taking the computerized exam.

Answering a question on the computerized exam is a three-part process. To start, you must click on the oval next to your answer choice. You can also click on any part of the answer beside that letter. Next, you must finish the answer by clicking on a button labeled "next," and finally, you must click the "answer confirm" oval. After you click "answer confirm," you cannot change your answer. If you decide to change an answer, you must do so by clicking on a different answer choice before you click the confirmation oval.

Time is important on the computerized test, just as it is on the paper test, so budget your time. Make sure that you allow enough time to complete each question without having to rush through the end of the test. Remember that some question types may take more time than others to answer. The reading comprehension questions are an example of this. Use your practice tutorial to help you gauge the amount of time you will need to complete the various question types.

Rushing is counterproductive. Remember, haste makes waste. Remind yourself that it is more valuable to you to answer one question correctly than to answer several questions incorrectly. Read each question carefully and eliminate answer choices that you know are wrong. Remember that the GRE may have a "best" answer instead of an absolutely "correct" answer. Do not waste time arguing with and second guessing yourself. After a reasonable amount of consideration, select the answer you think is best, confirm it, and move forward.

Make an effort to finish the entire test by budgeting your time wisely. Research shows that you are likely to receive a higher score by completing the entire test than you receive when you do not finish.

When considering time, remember that your 45-minute time period for the issue task on the analytical writing exam begins as soon as the two issue task choices appear. Do not use up too much of your time deciding which topic to address. Choose the topic, think about it, plan your response, and then write it. Make your "first draft" as perfect as you can without worrying excessively. The scoring team will treat your response as a first draft because of the time constraint that you are under, but you want it to be the best draft you can possibly produce.

> **Tip #41: This is a computerized test so if you do not use computers much, you should start.**

If you own a home computer, start finding things to do on it: Surf the net, send e-mails to your friends and family, or take practice GRE tests (we will talk more about that later). If you do not own a home computer, you can go to the public library and find more than a few to utilize.

> **Tip #42: The verbal section is just a matter of various parts that make up the whole.**

The verbal section of the GRE measures your ability to analyze and evaluate written material and also to synthesize information obtained from that written material. Reading comprehension passages in this section cover subjects in the areas of humanities, social sciences, and natural sciences. These passages are written for universal audiences, not for experts. It is more important to be able to read for information than to have advanced content knowledge about the topic. You will need to demonstrate your ability to understand antonyms and analogies and also to complete unfinished sentences and answer reading comprehension questions.

ANTONYMS

"Antonym" is the term used for a word that is the opposite of another word. In this section, the GRE measures your vocabulary and ability to reason from a given concept to its opposite. For example, the word *enervate* is an antonym of the word *invigorate*. *Enervate* means to reduce in strength. *Invigorate* means to impart vigor or vitality or to strengthen.

ANALOGIES

An "Analogy" is a relationship between two related things. In the GRE, you are determining what this relationship is and then applying it to the answer choices to find the identical relationship. When taking the GRE, you will be asked to read a pair of words and then to select another pair of words that express a similar relationship to that expressed by the first pair. Recognizing analogies shows that you are able to grasp the relationships between words and the concepts they represent and also that you can determine parallel relationships. You may have studied analogies in a format similar to the following: Shoe is to foot as tire is to _____. This example shows that analogies are often limited and that similarity between the two objects being compared does not exist at every level. After all, shoes are not frequently round. Many of the word pairs on the GRE are especially similar to each other, requiring you to go through a careful thought process before selecting your answer. The more you practice this skill before taking the test, the better your score will be.

SENTENCE COMPLETIONS

According to educator Laurie Rozakis, author of *Test Taking Strategies & Study*

Skills for the Utterly Confused, McGraw-Hill Professional, 2002, sentence completion questions test two areas of English language proficiency: the broad range of your vocabulary and your ability to understand the logic of sentences. The range of your vocabulary is measured by your ability to understand the meaning of sentences, and logic skills are measured by your ability to insert the correct word into a blank in a sentence. Here is an example:

By means of his_____, he managed to figure out the combination to the safe.

   A. Efficiency
   B. Routine
   C. Persuasion
   D. Persistence
   E. Fluency

READING COMPREHENSION

Reading comprehension is defined as your ability to provide accurate responses to questions concerning written language. The reading comprehension passages in the GRE measure your abilities to read with understanding and to analyze written passages from more than one perspective. All passages are taken from the areas of humanities, social sciences, and natural sciences, and they are written for the broad population, not for experts. GRE reading passages are presented in paragraph format, and every fifth line of the passage is numbered. Most passages have about 500 words.

> **Tip #43: Quantity matters too: Break down the math/quantitative section.**

Elementary mathematics, quantitative reasoning, and quantitative problem solving are tested in this section of the GRE. Questions cover arithmetic, algebra, geometry, and data analysis, and the number of questions covering each area is about the same.

The ETS® Web site, **www.ets.org**, offers the following definition and explanations of the four test areas:

Arithmetic questions may involve arithmetic operations, powers, operations on radical expressions, estimation, percent, absolute value, properties of integers (for example, divisibility, factoring, prime numbers, and odd and even integers), and the number line.

Algebra questions may involve rules of exponents, factoring and simplifying algebraic expressions, understanding concepts of relations and functions, equations and inequalities, solving linear and quadratic equations and inequalities, solving simultaneous equations, setting up equations to solve word problems, coordinate geometry (including slope, intercepts, and graphs of equations and inequalities), and applying basic algebra skills to solve problems.

Geometry questions may involve parallel lines, circles, triangles (including isosceles, equilateral, and 30, 60 and 90 degree triangles), rectangles, other polygons, area, perimeter, volume, the Pythagorean Theorem, and angle measure in degrees. The ability to construct proofs is not measured.

Data Analysis (Interpretation) questions may involve elementary probability, basic descriptive statistics (mean, median, mode, range, standard deviation, percentiles), and interpretation of data in graphs and tables (line graphs, bar graphs, circle graphs, frequency distributions).

After reading these explanations of the questions in the quantitative section, it should be obvious that you need to know what each operation is and how to perform it. If you discover that you need to review many of these operations, you must make a study plan with a timeline that allows you sufficient time to prepare for the exam.

Tip #44: Play the analytical game on the analytical writing section of the GRE.

The analytical writing section of the GRE tests your critical thinking skills via the means of your writing ability.

Most college papers require some kind of analysis, either as part of the pre-writing experience or as part of the organization of the paper itself. This section of the GRE is constructed to determine how well you can organize materials in your mind and communicate that organization in writing. Can you state a complex idea and then support it with the other information that you include in your writing? Can you analyze an argument and sustain a focused and coherent discussion on that topic?

You will need to pay careful attention to your grammar and style and to how you use words to transition from one topic to another. You must also acknowledge the originator, owner, publisher, and author of statement you include in your writing that are not yours originally. In other words, you must not plagiarize.

According to ETS®, (check out the Web site: **www.ets.org**) the analytical writing section consists of two separate analytical writing tests. One is a 45-minute perspective task and the other is a 30-minute argument task.

In the first section, you will be asked to select one of two issue topics. Both of these preselected topics state an opinion of an issue of broad interest. Your directions are to write about that topic from any perspective you choose, and to provide relevant reasons and examples to explain and support your point of view.

In the second section, only one argument is presented and your task is to critique that argument by discussing how well-reasoned you think it is. It is more important to consider the logical soundness of the argument than to express whether you agree with it.

Looking at this section of the GRE as a puzzle will reveal to you that these two writing tasks are complementary. The first task requires you to construct your own argument and the second requires you to critique someone else's argument. So in the first writing, you have to take a position and support it. In the second task, you have to assess a claim or position and evaluate it according to the evidence provided.

> **Tip #45: There have been some changes made to the GRE that may or may not affect you.**

According to ETS®, starting November 2007, GRE test takers could see either one question of the new verbal question type or one question of the new quantitative test type. ETS® also states that there is a possibility that GRE test takers will not see either new type of question.

The new verbal question type, Text Completion, is a complex form of sentence completion. Test takers must fill in two or three blanks within a passage with the correct vocabulary from separate multiple-choice lists.

The new quantitative question type, Numeric Entry, requires GRE test takers to manually enter an answer into an empty answer box. This means that the new question type does not involve multiple choices.

Do not panic. As these questions are first introduced, they will not count toward your score. Keep abreast of GRE test updates by checking in regularly with the ETS® Web site. Once a sufficient sample of data has been procured by ETS®, these question types will count toward a test taker's score.

> **Tip #46: Unfortunately, this is the time for experiments.**

The experimental section of your GRE will be a part of either the verbal or math section. According to ETS®, it will not be marked experimental or identified as experimental in any other way. ETS® also states that you will not know which section is the experimental section and may only notice that there is an experimental section by counting to see that an extra section of a certain type has been included in your exam. I can tell you from experience that both times I took the GRE, the experimental sections were clearly marked as such. Do not count on this happening during your exam; it may or may not. Also, do not worry, because experimental sections are not scored.

REVIEW: A LIST OF INFORMATION ABOUT THE STRUCTURE OF THE GRE

1. In addition to the scored sections, your GRE may include two non-scored sections, an unidentified experimental and identified research section.

2. The experimental and research sections are part of the process test designers use to "norm" a standardized test.

3. The test taking strategies that work best for the paper-based test are different from the strategies that work best for taking the computer-based test.

4. Accommodations are available for persons with disabilities.

5. If a test is valid, it measures what it claims to measure.

6. If a test is reliable, it yields the same results time after time.

7. Results of standardized tests are supposed to be predictable.

8. It is the predictability of the test that allows you to learn how to take it.

9. The predictability also allows colleges and universities to rely on the

scores as indicators of success in your first year of school.

10. Take a lighthearted approach to preparing for the GRE. Approach it as if it were a game or puzzle.

11. Take time to understand the structure of the exam in both the broad and specific structures of each section of the exam.

12. The analytical writing section is always given first.

13. The analytical writing section requires you to write two passages, the critical analysis of an issue and critique of an argument.

14. The verbal section has four parts: antonyms, analogies, sentence completion, and reading comprehension.

15. An antonym is a word with the opposite meaning from another word.

16. An analogy is a comparison of similarities.

17. Sentence completion tests vocabulary and understanding of sentence logic.

18. Reading comprehension refers to understanding and analyzing written passages.

19. The quantitative section is a math test.

20. The areas of quantitative measurement tested by the GRE are arithmetic, algebra, geometry, and data analysis.

21. After reviewing the structure of the GRE, you need to make a study plan with a timeline.

CHAPTER 7 HOMEWORK

1. Review the anatomy of the computer-based GRE.

2. List and define the various components of the verbal reasoning section of the GRE.

3. List and define the various components of the quantitative section of the GRE.

4. Write a one-paragraph summary about the analytical writing section of the GRE.

5. If you do not regularly use a computer, schedule time to begin doing so.

CHAPTER 8

How to Prepare for the Computerized Aspect of the GRE

> **Tip #47: Use a computer for anything and everything you can until your GRE test date.**

As discussed in Chapter 7, if you do not already use a computer on a frequent basis, you must begin to get accustomed to utilizing one as much as possible. When you sit down to take the computerized GRE, you will find yourself working on a computer for about three hours. This may come as a shock to you if you do not normally use computers. In the last chapter, I recommended that you start using a computer more frequently than you do now. I also suggested that you use it for anything and everything possible. Conduct research. Check your e-mail. Start reading the news online.

> **Tip #48: Start typing as much as you can before your GRE test date.**

The GRE begins with the analytical writing section. You are allowed 45 minutes to answer one question and 30 minutes to answer the next. You then receive a ten-minute break. Essentially, this means that you must type for one hour and fifteen minutes straight to commence your GRE. This is not an easy task. Have you ever actually typed anything for one hour and fifteen minutes straight?

You should include practicing analytical writing section sample questions in your study schedule. You might consider spending your "analytical writing section" study time in front of the computer, typing a response to a sample question. This will help you feel accustomed to typing for such an extended time, if you are not already.

You should also begin typing everything possible. Use e-mail instead of sending letters. Type out your weekly schedule or calendar.

Tip #49: If possible, schedule a visit to your testing center.

Do not be shy about doing everything that you want to make yourself feel comfortable on test day. Call the test center and ask if you can visit the facility in which your GRE will occur. This will accomplish a number of positive things: (1) When you arrive at the facility on test day, you will already know where it is and will not need to deal with the additional stress of "finding" the test center; (2) You will see what the building is like and how the room temperature is; (3) You may get to sneak a peek at the testing room. If you are not allowed to visit the testing facility or you are not permitted to look at the testing room, ask what types of computers the testing center uses for the GRE. Ask if the mouse is built into the keyboard or if it is separate. That way, you will know what to expect on test day.

CHAPTER **8** HOMEWORK

1. If you do not already use computers often, develop a plan for how to begin doing so. Start e-mailing your friends and family on a regular basis. Take practice tests for the GRE. Spend your "analytical writing section study time" by typing out responses to sample questions. Do what you can to use a computer for as long a period as possible, at least once or twice a week.

2. Practice typing for at least one hour and fifteen minutes at a time, since this is what you will need to do on your GRE test date. You can write a journal entry or practice typing a response to an actual analytical writing section sample question. Your best bet is to spend your time practicing with sample questions for the analytical writing section. You can access sample questions by completing the following steps:

   • Go to the Web site **www.ets.org**

   • Under "Tests," click on "GRE."

   • Under the section "Test Takers," click on "Practice for a GRE Test."

   • Click the bullet point for "GRE General Test."

   • You will now see a series of tabs. Click on "Writing Topics."

   • You can then select from "Pool of Issue Topics" or "Pool of Argument Topics."

3. Consider whether you want to visit your testing center prior to your test day. If so, schedule your visit. If you cannot visit the center or do not want to, call and ask about what types of computers they use for the GRE general test. Also, ask if the mouse is built into the keyboard, or if it is separate. That way, you will know what to expect on test day.

CHAPTER 9

How to Prepare for the Verbal Reasoning Section of the GRE

VERBAL ABILITY: "THE SKINNY"

- The verbal reasoning section consists of 30 questions.

- The four types of questions in this section are antonyms, analogies, sentence completions, and reading comprehension questions. You may also encounter a new question type that will be discussed at the end of this chapter.

- Your success on this section clearly depends on your verbal abilities. My advice, as a past GRE test taker, is to consider everything, except the reading comprehension section, as a vocabulary test. As for the reading comprehension section, consider it a test of how adept you are at finding information in a reading passage.

- The amount of time you spend on each question will vary. However, answering questions about long reading passages will most likely take you the most time. As a successful GRE test taker, what I remember most about the verbal section is that I needed the most time to answer the reading comprehension questions. Timing is critical. You must leave time to get through all of the reading comprehension questions.

- Do not sell yourself short on time by over thinking antonym or analogy questions to which you simply do not know the answer. If you do not know the meaning of the words, do your best to guess the word's meaning and then move on.

- If you are not sure how to answer a sentence completion question, it is reasonable to take some time with this if you know most of the vocabulary contained within the answer choices.

- Never spend too much time on one question. There are only 30 questions but there are also only 30 minutes within which to answer those questions. You have got to keep moving.

Here is the breakdown of the verbal section:

- Eight to ten antonym questions (vocabulary questions)

- Six to eight analogy questions (vocabulary questions)

- Five to seven sentence completion questions (vocabulary and logical reasoning skills questions)

- Six to ten reading comprehension questions (based on two to four passages)

- Possible text completion question (you may or may not see this question type)

When I first settled down to take the GRE several years ago, I felt discouraged from the start, particularly about the verbal reasoning section. I had heard through the grapevine that this section of the GRE tests skills that you have accumulated over a lifetime. I also knew that this section of the GRE placed a significant emphasis on vocabulary. I had heard several horror stories from other GRE test-takers who told me that words appeared on their GRE that they had never seen or heard of in their entire life. A few other people also told me that it was simply impossible to improve my vocabulary enough between the time I registered for the GRE and the time I would need to take it to actually have a valuable effect on my verbal section score.

Although this news was indeed discouraging, I was determined to study hard. I would like to encourage you to study hard for this section of the GRE just as hard as you will study for the quantitative section. Although it is true that both sections test skills accumulated over a lifetime, it does not mean that you cannot acquire most, if not all, of these skills and concepts before the test day. Do not let people, including the ETS® organization, discourage you. You should know that you can study hard, practice often, and score extremely well on this section of the GRE. I will now let you in on a little secret: When I initially took the GRE, I scored high enough to gain entrance into a master's program, but not a doctoral program. Even though my analytical writing score was outstanding, I needed a higher verbal reasoning score, since I wanted to begin a Ph.D. program in English, and English departments focus on the verbal section of the GRE. I ignored everyone who told me not to bother taking the test again. I studied hard, practiced often, and increased my score by a significant number of points. I primarily attribute that feat to the acquisition of vocabulary. The second most important factor in my massive score improvement was the fact that I practiced, practiced and then practiced some more. By the time test day rolled around, it was just another day of doing sentence completions, contemplating antonyms and analogies and reviewing reading comprehension passages — something I did nearly every day anyway.

As you answer each GRE question correctly, you will receive a harder question next. I never find it useful to focus on the scoring system of the GRE. If you do not know your vocabulary, I can assure you that the scoring system simply will not matter. If you have not practiced completing these portions of the verbal reasoning exam and if you have not practiced taking full-length verbal exams in one sitting, no strategies or tips will assist you in improving your score by any dramatic measure.

Concentrate on building your vocabulary first. That should be your number one priority. Then, work through the practice problems in this book. Go through the practice problems on the ETS® software you received after registering for the GRE. Then, start taking full-length practice tests. If you study and practice hard, you will achieve commendable results.

Tip #50: Vocabulary truly does do a brain good.

Increasing your vocabulary can significantly increase your GRE score. Unfortunately, a previous test taker told me that it was impossible for me to improve my vocabulary enough before test day enough to make a significant impact on my score. This is not true. Acquiring the definition and meaning of even eight to ten vocabulary words prior to test day could earn you several points on the test. You must begin to increase your vocabulary knowledge, no matter how much time you have before your test date. If you begin studying vocabulary now, and study it regularly over the course of your scheduled study time up until test day, you have an excellent chance of earning a higher GRE score.

Tip #51: Take a vocabulary list and break it down into sections.

The best way to learn vocabulary is to break a list down into sections and schedule when you will study each section. How you break things down into sections will inevitably depend on how much time stands between now and your GRE test date.

Flashcards can prove useful. If you decide to use flashcards, you have two options for doing so:

- Make your own with index cards.

- Purchase them.

This choice is up to your discretion, but I recommend the first option. Writing out vocabulary words and their definitions will help you commit words to memory. If you write out your own index cards, it can help you study.

Tip #52: Commit to studying certain sections of the vocabulary list at least six days a week until your exam date.

Here is an example of how you could break down your study plan:

Day 1: Study words that start with A–D from vocabulary list

Day 2: Study words that start with E–H

Day 3: Study words that start with I–M

Day 4: Study words that start with N–P

Day 5: Study words that start with Q–T

Day 6: Study words that start with U–Z

Day 7: Off

Alternatively, you might take day four off and rearrange the schedule. This is just an example. At the end of this chapter, you will find a vocabulary list that you can utilize. Feel free to break it down into sections, as suggested, and develop your study plan from there.

Tip #53: Start reading more than you do now.

I do not wish to discourage you, but based on my previous GRE test-taking experiences, even the experienced English major will find the reading comprehension sections of the GRE somewhat challenging and grueling, particularly since you must read these passages after you have written your analytical writing section for one hour and fifteen minutes straight, and have possibly also just taken a quantitative section (depending on how your own GRE test ends up being structured).

The reading passages on the GRE are dense. Due to recent changes, you will find that on some sections, certain passages are highlighted that you will want to focus your attention on in order to answer the questions. This is a new version of the reading comprehension question that ETS® began to introduce in January of 2008.

Regardless, depending on how much reading you do now, you may want to do more. When I was an undergraduate and graduate student, I did not do any reading outside what was required for my courses. This did not serve me well on the GRE, since the GRE reading comprehension passages covered subjects outside my field of study. While it is not necessary to possess knowledge about subjects outside your main course of studies, it can be helpful to read materials that cover a wide variety of subject matter.

Here are some examples of sources you could begin reading on a regular basis:

- Newspapers

- Scientific magazines

- Business journals

- Online articles about science or business

- Online articles about arts and humanities

It is fine to do your reading either in print or online. A combination of both will serve you the most since the reading comprehension section of the GRE will be computerized, just like the rest of the test.

> ## Tip #54: Start improving your reading comprehension.

Although reading more will help you on the GRE, you must also practice reading comprehension. Again, the reading comprehension passages on the GRE are dense. You may be somewhat tired by the time you get to these due to the stressful nature of the day and the fact that you have just finished the analytical writing section of the GRE. By the time your GRE test date rolls around, you want to be experienced in reading dense passages quickly and retaining information about what you just read. While it is true that the passage will remain on the screen for you to find the answers, and the highlighting of certain sections or the reference to specific lines in passages will help you, remember that the GRE is a timed test. You must answer the reading comprehension questions as quickly and efficiently as possible.

- **Tip:** Read newspaper, magazine, and journal articles outside your typical field of study, and then write a one- to two-paragraph summary about what you just read.

At the end of this chapter are practice questions for reading comprehension. You can complement the practice questions in this book with practice questions from the ETS® Web site. Instructions for how to do that will follow the sample reading comprehension questions at the end of this chapter.

> ## Tip #55: Start practicing analogies.

An analogy draws a comparison. Part of your GRE general test will contain questions that involve analogies. Since I am a successful, previous GRE test taker, I am going to let you in on a secret: *The analogy section of the GRE primarily tests your vocabulary skills.* While we will reveal strategies to "play the game" in terms of how to answer these questions, none of those tips or strategies will help you if you simply do not know the meaning of most of the words in the analogy questions. Therefore, building your vocabulary consistently throughout your GRE study process is absolutely essential to your success on answering the analogy questions on the GRE.

The second most critical step you can take to get these questions right and score higher on the GRE is to *practice*. You must practice drawing the inferences that analogies involve until it becomes second nature to you. Follow these steps to practice making the necessary connections between the two words presented to you in analogies:

- Determine the relationship between the two words by building a "bridge." How does the first word relate to the second, or vice versa?

  And example is, Porsche : Car

  "A Porsche is a type of car."

- Plug the answer choices into the relationship you have developed. In this case, the relationship is "is a type of."

- Adjust and make the relationship more precise, if necessary.

  Example: "A Porsche is a type of sports car."

At the end of this chapter, you will find sample questions to practice your analogy skills. You will also find directions on how to access additional practice questions. Listed below are some common "bridges" used in analogies. In each of these examples, X refers to the first word in a given analogy and Y refers to the second word.

- X is a type of Y (see above example)

- X is a subset of Y

- X and Y are synonyms

- X and Y are antonyms

- Something that is X has a tendency to Y

- An X type of person cannot be Y

- X is agreeable to Y

- X quality results in a Y type of person

- X is detected by Y

Tip #56: Decide what you are going to do if you do not know the meaning of one or both of the words in the analogy question.

If you are unsure how to answer the question, go through the answer choices and check their relationships. Do the words even have a relationship? Eliminate answer choices that do not even have a relationship.

Example: Magazine : Trumpet

Be careful about eliminating choices with the same relationship because there may be a nuance. If the relationship is truly identical (which is rare) then eliminate both choices; if there is a difference in the shade of meaning, then do not eliminate both choices.

If you do not know your vocabulary, you will have difficulty answering these questions correctly. Decide now not to spend excessive time trying to guess on questions to which you do not know the answer.

Tip #57: Start practicing for the sentence completion portion of the test.

The sentence completion portion of the GRE is another partial test of your vocabulary skills, although not as much as the analogy and antonym sections. If you are faced with a sentence completion question and do not know the meaning of the words in your answer choices, you have a problem, and that problem is based on a lack of vocabulary skills.

Therefore, building your vocabulary consistently throughout your GRE study process will help you answer more sentence completion questions correctly which will subsequently assist you in achieving a higher score on the GRE.

The second most critical step you can take in order to get these questions right and score higher on the GRE is to *practice*. I know sentence completion sounds so easy, and you might feel it is absurd to even consider the concept of practicing. If all of the sentence completion questions were easy, however, everyone would correctly answer them all when they take the GRE. Needless to say, people do not answer them all correctly.

Follow these steps to practice visualizing where a sentence is heading, and how you intend to complete it:

- Read the sentence carefully. Look for clues that point to where the sentence is heading. Most importantly, determine if the word(s) with which you must complete the sentence are positive or negative. This will help you eliminate incorrect answer choices.

Example: The _____ of her response to the question shocked and offended the reporter, who immediately backed down and _____ his approach to appease the interviewee.

In this example, it is clear that a reporter is interviewing someone. Whomever the reporter interviewed shocked and offended the reporter. Therefore, her response to the interviewer's question must have been negative, not positive. You now know that the word you need to fill in the first blank will have a negative connotation to it. Next, you can see from the structure of the sentence where it is headed. Once the reporter received the alarming and offensive response, he or she immediately backed down and attempted to appease the person whom he or she was interviewing. "Appease" is positive. You therefore now know that the answer to the second blank is a word with a positive — as opposed to a negative — connotation.

So, if the following were your answer choices for the above example, which should you choose?

    a. pleasantness…toughened
    b. alacrity…dimmed
    c. harshness…softened
    d. absurdity…intensified

Clearly, the first set of answers could not be correct. We already know from assessing the sentence that the first word should have a negative connotation. Since "pleasantness" has a positive connotation, we can immediately eliminate that entire answer.

Do you remember what I said about the importance of vocabulary? Do you know what alacrity means? If not, you might panic a bit, because you know from assessing the sentence that "dimmed" might be an appropriate choice for the second part of the sentence completion. If you do not know the meaning of alacrity, do not eliminate this choice. If you do know the meaning, you know that it has a positive connotation, and will therefore eliminate this answer choice altogether.

The third answer choice is clearly the best. The first word, "harshness," has a negative connotation and fits the sentence structure and logic. "Softened" also fits. Make a note of this answer choice.

You might briefly consider the fourth answer choice but should not. An "absurd" answer would not necessarily invoke an offended response from someone. Moreover, "intensified" does not necessarily have a positive connotation to it.

If you knew the meaning of alacrity, you quickly and efficiently identified answer choice three as the correct one.

If you did not know the meaning of alacrity, you were left to contemplate whether the second or third answer choices are correct. Here is what you know: The third answer choice is a perfect fit. Go back to the second answer choice. Is "dimmed" the appropriate word for fine-tuning a response? "Dimming" involves lighting, right? Your best guess, in this instance, is answer choice number three. Remember that ETS® wants the best answer, even if more than one answer appears possibly correct.

Tip #58: Start practicing with antonyms.

Can you guess what the antonym portion of the GRE tests? This section is truly another test of your *vocabulary skills*. Clearly, if you know the meaning of the word in question, you will not likely experience much difficulty in determining its opposite meaning. If, however, you see a word and do not know its definition, you will have difficulty identifying its antonym. Therefore, building your vocabulary consistently throughout your GRE study process will help you answer more antonym questions correctly which will subsequently assist you with achieving a higher score on the GRE.

The second critical step you can take to get these questions right and score higher on the GRE is to continue exercising your skills with practice questions. Again, though, if you do not even have a remote idea of the meaning of the word in question, you will experience a tremendous challenge when attempting to determine its antonym. There are few, if any, strategies or "tricks" that can get you out of a sticky situation like that.

When you do know the meaning — or at least have a general idea — of what a word on an antonym question means, follow these steps to determine its opposite, or antonym:

- Define the root word. If you cannot define it but it seems familiar, make a mental note of the general idea of what the word means. If you cannot accomplish that, see if you can accomplish anything. Is the word positive in connotation? Negative?

- Think about the opposite meaning of the word.

- Go to the answer questions and find the word that most closely fits the opposite. Again, you must know the meaning of the answer choices (just like you should know the meaning of the root word) to best answer these questions.

Example:

ALACRITY:

    a. enthusiasm
    b. disinterest
    c. inspiration
    d. loyalty
    e. aversion

All right, step number-one: Do you know what alacrity means? If so, you know that it refers to eagerness and enthusiasm. Therefore, answer choices one and two are clearly synonyms and can be eliminated. The fifth answer choice is unrelated and should be removed as well. You are now left with the third and fourth answer choices. Which fits best? Is aversion (opposition) a better antonym for eagerness than disinterest? Disinterest seems to imply more of a neutral connotation than a negative. Therefore, you know that the third answer choice is best.

If you do not know what alacrity means, do you know whether it is positive or negative? If you know that it is positive, you know that the word's antonym will be negative. You can therefore narrow down your answer choices to the third and fourth choices: aversion and disinterest. Since you know that aversion has more of a negative connotation than disinterest, you will choose this answer.

If you do not know what alacrity means, do not waste an excessive amount of time on the question. There are no tips or strategies to circumvent such a situation. Many studies have shown that "C" or the third answer choice, when guessed, is most often correct. In this case, that choice would work in your favor.

- **Tip:** On antonyms and analogies the answer choices will always have the same part of speech as the root word. For instance, the root word "milk" might have two possible parts of speech. It might be a noun, as in the milk that you drink, or it could be a verb, as in to milk or extract fully. All of the answer choices will have the same part of speech as each other and as the root word, so if you are unsure which part of speech the root word has, you can find your answer in the choices.

> **Tip #59: Practice taking entire verbal reasoning sections of the GRE all at one time, and take at least one test per week.**

Once you have consistently practiced reading comprehension, analogies, sentence completions, and antonyms, the best thing you can do is practice all of these question types in succession, since that is how the actual GRE is structured. Take as many practice tests of the entire verbal section as you can. The ETS® Web site offers practice tests. Moreover, when you register for the GRE, ETS® will send you software that includes two full-length verbal reasoning tests and full-length GREs. You can also purchase other prep books on the market to complement your studies. Most of these books will come with a CD, which will also have practice tests on them. *Practice, practice, practice.*

CASE STUDY: RONALD MEDVIN

BA, MAT
9769 Montague Street
Tampa, FL 33626
813-289-7700
ronald.medvin@sdhc.k12.fl.us
Ronald Medvin, Instructor, GRE Verbal
Preparation: University of South Florida

Test Preparation

As one who has taught the GRE Verbal Preparation course for four years, I often meet students who are in a state of panic when they are faced with taking the verbal examination. I tell them that this is not a course that will automatically guarantee success in six weeks. There is no magic bullet that this, or any course, will provide. As much as some students don't wish to hear this, success simply depends on practice and more practice. While there are strategies that students can learn, this test is primarily a vocabulary test.

I have found that the more students read, the better their vocabulary, and the better their score on the test. Believe it or not, the GRE is very much like the SAT® you took in high school, only with more difficult vocabulary and more "distractors."

During the course, I teach students to always read all the answer choices, as the most common errors are made due to carelessness and misreading. There are other strategies, of course.

However, no matter how many strategies we cover in class, *if students do not practice outside class, taking the class itself and expecting dramatic results will prove to be disappointing.* This means studying vocabulary lists in the texts, taking GRE practice tests over and over again, and writing and rewriting issue and argument essays until you feel comfortable writing coherently in one 30 minute section and one 45 minute section. Also, if nothing else, make sure you take practice tests on the computer, for taking a multiple choice test on a computer can be a nerve-wracking experience if you have never done so previously.

You will probably take the GRE test more than once. You will probably understand, after your first experience, why I keep stressing practice. It is not what many students want to hear, but there are no shortcuts. As in anything else that truly matters, working hard to achieve success is the only answer.

500+ Practice GRE Vocabulary Words

A

abase: (v.) to humiliate, cause to feel shame; (v.) to hurt the pride of

abash: (v.) to embarrass; to cause to be embarrassed

abate: (v.) to make less active or intense; (v.) to become less in intensity

abdicate: (v.) to give up power

aberration: (n.) an aberrant state or condition; (n.) a disorder in a person's mental state; an optical phenomenon which results from the failure of a mirror or lens to produce a good image

abet: (v.) to assist or encourage, often in the case of wrongdoing; (v.) to support, uphold, or maintain; (v.) to contribute to the commission of an offense

abeyance: (n.) a temporary suspension or cessation; (n.) a temporary suppression

abhor: (v.) to find repugnant, or to shrink back with dislike or horror

abjure: (v.) to reject something; (v.) to retract an oath; (v.) to recant

aboriginal: (n.) an original inhabitant of any land; (n.) an animal or plant native to the region

abortive: (adj.) failing to accomplish an original intent or goal; (adj.) imperfectly formed or developed; (n.) something that is born prematurely; (adj.) made from the skin of a still-born animal

abscond: (v.) to run away, often taking someone or something along; (v.) to hide, withdraw or be concealed

absolve: (v.) to release from moral wrongdoing; (v.) to grant remission of a sin

abstain: (v.) to refrain from engaging in a certain act; (v.) to voluntarily refrain from, especially when having to do with an act involving the appetite or senses

abstemious: (adj.) sparing in consumption of, especially in relation to food and drink; (adj.) marked by moderation in indulgence

abyss: (n.) a gulf or pit that is either bottomless or which possesses an unfathomable and inconceivable depth; (n.) infinite time

abysmal: (adj.) boundless and vast; (adj.) unfathomable

accede: (v.) to give into or yield to someone else's wishes or desires; (v.) to be in accordance with; to agree

acclivity: (n.) an upward grade or slope, on the earth

accolade: (n.) to praise; (n.) a symbol that signifies distinction or approval; (n.) a ceremony that was formerly used to bestow knighthood

accoutre: (v.) to provide with military equipment

accretion: (n.) an increase brought about by natural growth; (n.) an increase in a beneficiary's awarded portion of an estate

acetic: (adj.) containing or relating to acetic acid; vinegary smell or taste, particularly in relation to wine

acidulous: (adj.) tasting sour like

acme: (n.) the highest degree or level attainable, the highest point of something; mature age; (n.) the crisis or height of a disease

acquiescence: (n.) acceptance without resistance or protest; assent or submission; (n.) in criminal law: submission to an injury by the injured party

acquiescent: (adj.) willing to carry out someone else's orders or wishes without any protest or dissent; (adj.) submissive

actuate: (v.) to trigger a reaction or to move and incite to action; (v.) to carry out or perform

adapt: (v.) to modify or change to suit a new purpose or conditions; (v.) to conform one's own self to new conditions or a new environment

addiction: (n.) a situation in which someone is dependent on something that is physiologically and/or psychologically habit forming, particularly in relation to alcohol or drugs

adhere: (v.) to be in accordance with or compatible with; to carry out a plan without deviation; (v.) to come into close contact with; to be a devoted supporter or follower, in a religious sense

adipose: (adj.) composed of animal fat

admonish: (v.) to counsel in relation to one's negative behavior; (v.) to warn against strongly; (v.) to take to task

adulterate: (adj.) mixed with impurities; (v.) to corrupt or debase by adding a foreign substance

adumbration: (n.) a rough summary of the main aspects of an argument or theory; providing vague indications of something in advance

adversity: (n.) a state of affliction or misfortune; extreme challenge or hardship; (n.) a stroke of excessively bad fortune

advert: (v.) to give heed to; (v.)

to make a subversive or overt reference to

advocate: (n.) a person who stands for and/or pleads for a cause, idea or person; (n.) a lawyer who pleads a case in a court of law; (v.) to push for or recommend something; (v.) to argue in favor of

aerie: (n.) a lofty nest of a bird of prey, such as an eagle or hawk; (n.) a habitation of high altitude

aesthetic: (adj.) relating to beauty or good taste; (n.) a specialty in philosophy that relates to what is beautiful and how humans respond to art and beauty in the world

affable: (adj.) exemplifying warmth and friendliness; (adj.) gracious and mild

affected: (adj.) acted on or influenced; (adj.) experiencing an emotional impact

aggrandize: (v.) to add details to; to increase in power; (v.) to make something appear exceedingly great or exalted

affiliation: (n.) association in

or with a professional or societal group; (n.) connection in terms of descent (from birth)

affinity: (n.) the force which attracts atoms and binds them together in the formation of a molecule; (n.) a close connection marked by shared interests or similarities; an intrinsic resemblance between persons and/ or things; a natural attraction to or feeling of kinship for; (adj.) kinship by marriage or adoption

affray: (n.) a noisy fight or quarrel; the act of disturbing someone; fear or fright

agape: (adj.) with the mouth wide open due to wonder or awe; (n.) a religious meal shared as a sign of fellowship, love, and respect

aggregate: (n.) gathered or having a tendency to gather in a mass or whole; (n.) the whole amount; (v.) to gather in a mass or whole

aghast: (adj.) struck with fear, disgust, dismay and/or horror

agnostic: (adj.) uncertain of all claims relating to knowledge; (n.) a person who doubts the truth of religion and/or does not hold a particular view or perspective on the existence or nonexistence of God

alacrity: (n.) cheerful readiness, promptness, eagerness

agrarian: (adj.) agricultural or relating to farms and agriculture, fields or lands; (n.) a person in favor of an equal division of property

alchemy: (n.) a forerunner of chemistry, originating from the medieval era; (n.) the manner in which two individuals relate to each other

alias: (n.) a temporarily assumed name, other than one's real name

allay: (v.) to lessen the intensity of; (v.) to calm; to quench, particularly in terms of thirst

allege: (v.) to report or accuse

alleviate: (v.) to provide physical relief, particularly from pain; (v.) to make easier

allocate: (v.) to distribute according to a particular plan; (v.) to set aside

aloof: (adj.) to be somewhat at a distance or apart from a crowd; detached or reserved in mannerisms

altercation: (n.) a quarrel or argument

amalgamation: (n.) the mixing or blending together of various elements, including races or societies; (n.) the result of such blending; (n.) the combination of two or more commercial companies

ambiguous: (adj.) unclear; (adj.) uncertain in nature; open to more than one interpretation

ameliorate: (v.) to make something or someone better

amenable: (adj.) willing to comply; (adj.) responsible to a higher authority

amnesia: (n.) a partial or total loss of memory

amnesty: (n.) a period during which criminals are exempt from punishment; (n.) a warrant that grants release from a previously meted out punishment; (v.) the official act of liberating someone, in a legal sense; to grant a pardon

amortize: (v.) to gradually liquidate; to clear off or extinguish, particularly in relation to a debt

amuck: (adj.) in a murderous tumult; wildly or without self-control

amulet: (n.) a piece of jewelry thought to protect an individual against evil

anachronism: (n.) something located during a time when it could not have actually existed or occurred; (n.) an artifact that belongs to a different time period; (n.) a person displaced in time

analgesia: (n.) the absence of the sense of pain, but with consciousness still in tact

analogy: (n.) an insinuation that if things agree in one respect, they agree in others; (n.) a comparison drawn to show similarities

anarchy: (n.) a state of disorder and lawlessness, resulting from a lack of or failure in government

anesthetic: (adj.) characterized by a lack of sensibility; (n.) a drug that temporarily causes loss of bodily sensations

animus: (n.) a feeling of ill-will that arouses hostility or animosity

annul: (v.) to declare void or invalid, particularly in the case of a marriage, law or contract; (v.) to eliminate the existence of

antagonism: (n.) hostility that results in conflict, resistance or opposition; (n.) the condition of being an opposing force or factor in a situation or system

antipathy: (n.) a strong feeling of hostility or dislike

apex: (n.) the highest point of something, particularly in the case of a triangle, cone or pyramid

aplomb: (n.) poise; (n.) self-confidence

apocalyptic: (adj.) relating to the apocalypse; involving or implying doom and ultimate devastation; (adj.) of a prophetic nature

apostate: (n.) a person who has abandoned his or her political party, religion, or cause

appease: (v.) to bring pacification or peace to someone who is upset or contentious; (v.) to satisfy or relieve

appellation: (n.) a formal name or title; (n.) the act of naming (officially)

apprehend: (v.) to arrest or take an individual into custody; (v.) to mentally grasp a concept or principle

apprehensive: (adj.) anxious or fearful about the future; (adj.) capable of understanding concepts quickly

aptitude: (n.) an aptitude for learning; a talent; (n.) quickness in understanding, intelligence

archives: (n.) a collection of records, particularly related to the history of records of an institution

ardor: (n.) a feeling of strong eagerness or enthusiasm; an intense feeling of love; (n.) feelings of warmth and affection

arraign: (v.) to command a prisoner or free person accused of a crime to appear in court to answer a charge

arrant: (adj.) downright or utter, particularly unqualified

artifact: (n.) man-made object

artifice: (n.) a clever trick; (n.) skill or cunningness

asceticism: (n.) the principles and practices of an ascetic, particularly in relation to extreme self-denial; (n.) self-restraint practiced in relation to a religious or spiritual doctrine or practice that claims the renunciation of worldly pleasures allows one to achieve a higher spiritual state of being

ascribe: (v.) to attribute to; (v.) to assign a quality or characteristic

askance: (v.) to view with an oblique glance; (v.) to regard with suspicion

askew: (adj.) turned or twisted toward one side

aspiration: (n.) a desire or will to succeed; a cherished desire; (n.) an expulsion of breath during the active process of speech; the act of inhaling or drawing in air

assail: (v.) to violently attack; to criticize; (v.) to cause trouble to

assimilate: (v.) to learn, understand and incorporate information; (v.) to adjust or become adjusted to a different environment; to absorb (food)

assuage: (v.) to make something less intense or severe; (v.) to satisfy or appease, to pacify or calm

astringent: (adj.) causing the contraction of body tissue; severe or harsh; (n.) an drug or lotion that draws pores together and/or causes their contraction

astute: (adj.) rapid to apprehend or understand

atrocity: (n.) a behavior, event or incident that is characterized by cruelty and wickedness; (n.) an act of extreme cruelty

attrition: (n.) a constant wearing down caused by friction; (n.) a gradual decrease in strength, due to consistent stressful conditions; a gradual reduction in membership or personnel; (n.) repentance for a sin, motivated by the fear of God and punishment

augment: (v.) to make something larger in size or quantity

augury: (n.) the art of foretelling the future by means of various sings; (n.) an omen from which the future if foretold

auspicious: (adj.) related to positive and favorable circumstances; (adj.) marked by success and prosperity

austere: (adj.) stern, in terms of character or disposition; (adj.) strict or severe in discipline; lacking adornment or decoration

autonomous: (adj.) not controlled by other individuals or organizations; (adj.) independent in mind and judgment

avatar: (n.) the animal or human incarnation of a Hindu deity, particularly Vishnu; (n.) an embodiment of a quality or concept; a temporary manifestation of an ongoing entity

aver: (v.) to officially assert as a fact; (v.) to justify, qualify or prove

avouch: (v.) to attest to or declare the validity of; (v.) to confirm; to accept responsibility for an action; to confess

avow: (v.) to openly acknowledge; (v.) to positive and undoubtedly profess

axiom: (n.) a universally recognized truth; (n.) a seemingly self-evident principle

B

baffle: (v.) to frustrate someone, by perplexing or confusing them; (v.) to impede the force or movement of

baleful: (adj.) harmful, threatening or deadly

baneful: (adj.) causing distress, death or ruin

barrage: (n.) a prolonged attack of words or blows; a curtain of (military) artillery fire to prevent enemy forces from moving or to make way for one's own forces; (n.) a man-made barrier in a stream or river

batten: (n.) a sawed strip of wood or flooring; (trans. verb) to fasten canvas over the hatches, especially in preparation for a storm; (v.) to grow fat

bauble: (n.) a decorative or showy but worthless object

beguile: (v.) to mislead by trickery or deception

beholden: (adj.) obliged to feel grateful for or owing thanks

beleaguer: (v.) to besiege by encircling; to harass or beset with difficulties

belittle: (v.) to make someone feel little or less important, to slight someone

benevolent: (adj.) doing or intending to do good

benison: (n.) a benediction

berate: (v.) to severely rebuke or scold; (v.) to criticize, slate

bestial: (adj.) beast-like in behavior, brutish

biennial: (adj.) occurring every two years; (adj.) lasting or living for two years

billingsgate: (n.) abuse, foul or vulgar language

bivouac: (n.) a temporary encampment (usually of military soldiers) exposed out in the open with only tents or little shelter

blandish: (v.) to flatter, coax or persuade

blasphemous: (adj.) irreverent or profane, particularly in relation to a religious subject

bleak: (adj.) unsheltered and exposed to wind and cold; (adj.) cold, cutting and harsh; gloomy; (adj.) not hopeful

bode: (v.) to predict or announce in advance

bogus: (adj.) not veritable or genuine

boorish: (adj.) rude; awkward, ill-mannered

bootless: (adj.) useless, without benefit

brackish: (adj.) somewhat salty, as might be the waters near a sea; having an displeasing taste; nauseous

breach: (n.) a failure to follow through on or complete the agreement and terms of a contract or law; (n.) an opening created by a breakthrough (in a wall); (n.) a break in amicable relations

bristle: (n.) any short, stiff or prickly hair of an animal or plant; (intrans. verb) to become stiff and erect; (n.) to show anger, irritation or outrage; (n.) to be thickly covered with

brusque: (adj.) abrupt and rough use of language or manner of speech

bumptious: (adj.) arrogant, excessively conceited, forward

burlesque (n.) any comic or satirical imitation (for example) in the form of writing, theater or a parody, intending to mock; (adj.) bawdy

burnish: (v.) to polish or to make shiny

C

cabal: (n.) a group of plotters

or intriguers with conspiratorial intentions; (n.) a secret scheme or plot

cache: (n.) a hiding place, especially in the ground for ammunition, food or treasures; (n.) anything so hidden; (v.) to put in a cache

caliber: (n.) degree of capacity or competence

calumniate: (v.) to make false and malicious statements about

candor: (n.) the state or quality of being open, honest, straightforward, open and sincere in communication; (n.) freedom from bias

canter: (n.) an easy-going gallop; (v.) to move or ride at a canter

capitulate: (v.) to surrender often after negotiation of terms

captious: (adj.) characterized by a disposition to find out and point trivial faults; (adj.) intended to entrap or confuse

carnage: (n.) the slaughter of numerous people; (n.) those slain in battle

carping: (adj.) characterized by trivial fault-finding

caste: (n.) any of the social or subclasses of traditional Hindu society, such as the Brahman or Sudra castes; a social class distinct from others and characterized by hereditary rank, profession or wealth; (n.) a social position conferred on someone based on a system of castes

cataclysm: (n.) any violent upheaval, particularly of a political or social nature; (n.) an extensive flood

catalyst: (n.) (in chemistry), a substance that causes a chemical reaction without itself being affected; (n.) a person or thing that brings about or precipitates change; (n.) a person or event that precipitates a process or change

cathartic: (adj.) physically or emotionally purging in nature; (adj.) therapeutic

Catholic: (adj.) of or pertaining to the Catholic church; a member of the Catholic church; (adj.) of a broad, liberal or comprehensive scope

cavil: (v.) to raise trivial objections; (n.) a trivial or annoying objection

celibate: (n.) one who abstains from sexual relations with others; (n.) an individual who remains unmarried

centrifugal: (adj.) moving or directed outward from the center; (n.) a rotating, perforated drum that holds materials to be separated in a machine

centripetal: (adj.) moving or directed toward an axis or center; (adj.) tending or directed toward centralization

cessation: (n.) a temporary discontinuance

chameleon: (n.) any of the Old World lizards which can change color; (n.) a changeable or inconstant person

charlatan: (n.) a person who pretends to have more knowledge or skill than he or she actually possesses; (n.) a cont artist or fake

chary: (adj.) cautious or careful; (adj.) fastidious; sparing

chastise: (v.) to criticize severely; (v.) to discipline through corporal punishment

chide: (v.) to express disapproval of, to harass or reproach

chimerical: (adj.) fantasy, unreal or imaginary; (adj.) highly unrealistic

chronic: (adj.) constant and habitual; (adj.) lasting a long time, especially pertaining to a disease

circuitous: (adj.) indirect or roundabout

circumlocution: (n.) an indirect or roundabout way of speaking

citadel: (n.) a fortress in a commanding position in or near a city; a fortified place

claustrophobia: (n.) a excessive fear of being in closed or confined spaces

clemency: (n.) a willingness to lessen the severity of a given punishment; (n.) an official act of mercy or forgiveness

cliché: (n.) an overused expression or idea; (n.) a person whose behavior is predictable

coalesce: (v.) to fuse, grow or mix together

cogent: (adj.) believable, convincing or persuasive by clear and forcible presentation; (adj.) to the point

cognomen: (n.) a family or surname

cohere: (v.) to hold together in a mass that resists separation; (v.) to cause to form a united, aesthetically uniform whole

collaborate: (v.) to work together or cooperate; (v.) join forces

colloquial: (adj.) characteristic of ordinary conversation, rather than formal speech or writing

comatose: (adj.) of, related to or in a coma; (adj.) characterized by lethargy

commensurate: (adj.) of the same extent or duration; corresponding in size or degree, proportionate; (adj.) measurable by a common standard

compatible: (adj.) capable of

existing harmoniously; (adj.) capable of integration with other elements in a system without any additional required modifications

compendium: (n.) a complete, short summary; (n.) a list or collection of various items

complement: (n.) something that completes or makes something else whole; (n.) a quantity that completes anything; (n.) either of two parts, needed to complete the whole

compliment: (n.) an expression of praise (v.) to give someone praise or accolades

compliant: (adj.) disposed or willing to comply

conciliate: (v.) to overcome the mistrust of; (v.) to regain or attempt to regain friendship; (v.) to attempt to reconcile

concomitant: (adj.) existing or occurring with something else

congeal: (v.) to solidify or jell by freezing; coagulate

conjecture: (n.) the expression of or formulation of a theory without

sufficient evidence or proof; (v.) to guess or formulate a theory without sufficient evidence or proof

connotation: (n.) an idea or meaning suggested or associated with a word or thing; (n.) the set of associations implied by a word, in addition to its implicit meaning

contentious: (adj.) tending to cause argument or strife; (adj.) characterized by argument or controversy

controvert: (v.) to be resistant to, to raise arguments against, to oppose

contumacious: (adj.) willfully obstinate or stubbornly disobedient; (adj.) insubordinate

conveyance: (n.) the act of conveying or transmission

copious: (adj.) large in quantity or number; (adj.) having or yielding a plentiful supply; (adj.) exhibiting abundance

corporeal: (adj.) of or relating to the body; (adj.) of a material nature

corpulent: (adj.) large or bulky in body

countermand: (v.) to cancel or reverse an order or transmission previously issued; (n.) cancellation of an order or command

cower: (v.) to cringe, crouch or curl up in fear, to show fear

coy: (adj.) tending to avoid people or social situations; (adj.) shy or modest in a flirtatious manner; (adj.) stubbornly unwilling to make a comment

craven: (adj.) cowardly, spineless; (n.) a coward

credence: (n.) acceptance as truth or valid; trustworthiness; (n.) recommendation, credentials

crone: (n.) an ugly and withered woman, a hag

crotchety: (adj.) grouchy in nature or characterized by whimsical and odd notions

cryptic: (adj.) mysterious in meaning, puzzling; (adj.) secret, occult

cull: (v.) to pick out from others, select; (v.) to remove rejected members or parts from

culmination: (n.) the highest point or degree of completion

curmudgeon: (n.) an ill-tempered person

curtail: (v.) to cut short; (v.) reduce, diminish

cynic: (n.) a person with a pessimistic outlook and who believes that most people are solely motivated by selfishness

D

dank: (adj.) unpleasantly moist or humid; (adj.) damp, chilly

dastard: (n.) a mean-spirited, conniving coward

dearth: (n.) a lack, scarcity or inadequate supply

debacle: (n.) a breakup or dispersion; (n.) downfall; (n.) a complete collapse or failure; (n.) a violent rush of waters or ice

debonair: (adj.) having a sophisticated charm; (adj.) courteous and gracious; carefree

decimate: (v.) to destroy a great

number or proportion of; (v.) to select and kill every tenth person of a group

decrepit: (adj.) weakened or destabilized by old age; (adj.) worn out by extensive use

defile: (v.) to make foul, dirty or unclean; (v.) to violate the chastity of; (v.) to make impure or defile

deign: (intr. v.) to deem something inappropriate to one's dignity (tr. verb) condescend; (v.) give or grant

demean: (v.) to degrade, particularly in terms of social status or dignity

demotic: (adj.) of or relating to the common people of a given area or region

denizen: (n.) an inhabitant or resident; (n.) someone who frequents a given place

denotation: (n.) the act of denoting, that which gives an indication of or points to something, like a symbol or sign; (n.) the most specific meaning of a given word

deplete: (v.) to reduce or eliminate in supply

deprecatory: (adj.) expressing criticism or disapproval of; (adj.) uncomplimentary

depreciate: (v.) to reduce the value or price of

deride: (v.) to laugh at in a contemptuous or scornful manner

descry: (v.) to see something by looking carefully at it, to discover or perceive

desecrate: (v.) to violate the sacredness of a given object or place

desultory: (adj.) not having any set plan; (adj.) moving or jumping about from one subject to the next

dexterous: (adj.) skillful with the use of one's hands; (adj.) having mental skill

diatribe: (n.) a bitter, sharp or abusive attack or criticism

dichotomy: (n.) division into two part or regions

digress: (v.) to stray away from the main subject, particularly in writing or speech

dilettante: (n.) a dabbler in an art or particular field of knowledge, for the sole sake of amusement

dire: (adj.) causing or involving fright and suffering; (adj.) urgent and desperate

disabuse: (v.) to free from a falsehood or misconception

disheveled: (adj.) in disorder; (adj.) unkempt; (adj.) disarranged

disparage: (v.) to speak of in a disrespectful or condescending way; (v.) to reduce in respect or rank

dispirited: (adj.) in low spirits; (adj.) lacking enthusiasm

dissipate: (v.) to drive away or disperse; (v.) to bring about the loss of energy

dissolute: (adj.) lacking in moral restraint

diurnal: (adj.) relating to a 24-hour period, daily; (adj.) occurring or active during the daytime

doddering: (adj.) shaking or trembling from old age; (adj.) trembling

dolorous: (adj.) exhibiting grief, pain and sorry

dolt: (n.) a person who lacks bright mental capacity

dotage: (n.) a decline of mental faculties; (n.) foolish affection

doughty: (adj.) marked by courage and braveness

dross: (n.) waste; (adj.) worthless or trivial matter

drudgery: (n.) menial and distasteful work

duplicity: (n.) deceitfulness in speech or conduct, speaking or acting in two different ways

durance: (n.) incarceration or imprisonment

E

ebullient: (adj.) overflowing with enthusiasm or excited; (adj.) bubbling up like a boiling liquid

ecstasy: (n.) intense joy or delight; (n.) a trace or state of emotion so intense that one is carried beyond self-control

edify: (v.) to instruct or benefit, (v.) particularly in relation to intellectual or spiritual matters; to uplift

effeminate: (adj.) having feminine qualities or characteristics; (adj.) characterized by excessive refinement or weakness

effigy: (n.) a crude person or figure which represents a hated person or group; (n.) a likeness or image, particularly of a person

efflorescent: (adj.) bursting into flower; (adj.) flowering

effusion: (n.) a unrestrained expression of emotion; (n.) flow under pressure, such as the escape of bodily fluid from vessels into the tissues or a cavity

egress: (n.) the act of coming or going out; (n.) the right to leave or go out; (n.) a path or opening for the purposes of going out (v.) to go out

elucidate: (v.) to make lucid or clear, to throw light upon; (v.) to explain or provide clarification

elusive: (adj.) tending to elude capture, comprehension or perception; (adj.) difficult to define or describe

emancipate: (v.) to free from oppression or restraint; (v.) (as a legal term) to release a child from the control of parents or a guardian

embellish: (v.) to make beautiful by ornamentation; (v.) to decorate; (v.) to add false and fictitious detail to

emend: (v.) to edit or change a text; (v.) to correct, or free from faults or errors

eminent: (adj.) of high rank in station or quality; (adj.) outstanding in character or performance; (adj.) towering or standing above others

emollient: (adj.) softening and soothing, especially to the skin; making less harsh or abrasive

enamored: (adj.) inspired by love; captivated; (adj.) marked by foolish or unreasoning fondness

encroach: (v.) to advance beyond proper, established or usual limits; (v.) to trespass upon the domain, property or rights of another individual or organization

endue: (v.) to gift or provide with a quality or trait; (v.) to put on (a piece of clothing)

engross: (v.) to exclusively occupy; (v.) absorb; (v.) to acquire most or all of a commodity or market

enhance: (v.) to make greater in beauty, effectiveness or value; (v.) to provide with improved or enhanced features

ennui: (n.) listlessness and dissatisfaction; (n.) boredom

enthrall: (v.) to captivate or interest; (v.) to enslave

entity: (n.) something that exists as a particular unit; (n.) the fact of existence, being; (n.) the existence of something considered separate from its properties

ephemeral: (adj.) lasting a very short time; transitory; (adj.) lasting only one day

epilogue: (n.) a short poem or speech directed to the audience, given at the end of a play; (n.) the performer who delivers such a poem or speech; a short addition or concluding section at the end of a literary work

epitaph: (n.) an inscription on a monument or tombstone in memory of the person buried there within; (n.) a commemoration for someone who has died

equable: (adj.) free from many changes or variations; (adj.) uniform

equanimity: (n.) the quality of being calm, composed, even-tempered and stable

errant: (adj.) roving; (adj.) straying from the appropriate course of action or standards

eschew: (v.) to abstain or keep away from; (v.) to shun or avoid

estranged: (adj.) displaying a feeling or the characteristic of alienation; (adj.) kept in or at a distance

ethereal: (adj.) characterized by insubstantiality, intangible; (adj.) of the celestial spheres

eugenic: (adj.) of or related to bringing about improvements in offspring; (adj.) having quality, inherited characteristics

evanescent: (adj.) vanishing, fading; (adj.) fleeting; (adj.) tending to become imperceptible

evasive: (adj.) tending or seeking to avoid; (adj.) elusive

ewer: (n.) a pitcher with a wide spout

exacerbate: (v.) to make worse or increase the severity of; (v.) to irritate or exasperate a person

excision: (n.) the surgical act of removal

excoriate: (v.) to severely berate or denounce (verbally); (v.) to physically strip off or remove the skin from

exegesis: (n.) a critical analysis or explanation of a text

exemplary: (adj.) commendable

exiguous: (adj.) scanty or meager

exodus: (n.) a departure that usually involves a large number of people

expedite: (v.) to hasten or speed up the progress of; (v.) to quickly accomplish; (v.) to issue or dispatch a document or letter

expiate: (v.) to atone or make amends for, particularly in relation to a given individual's crimes

expunge: (v.) to erase or obliterate; (v.) to destroy

extol: (v.) to lift up; (v.) to praise highly

extricate: (v.) to disentangle; (v.) to disengage from a difficult situation

extrinsic: (adj.) not essential or inherent qualities; (adj.) outward or external

exude: (v.) to discharge or emit; (v.) to exhibit

F

fabricate: (v.) to make up or create; (v.) to concoct in an effort to deceive someone

facile: (adj.) easily accomplished or attained; (adj.) expressing yourself readily or clearly

fain: (adv.) gladly, willingly; (adj.) content, willing; (v.) to wish or desire

fastidious: (adj.) displaying careful attention to detail; (adj.) difficult to please; (adj.) excessively meticulous

faux pas: (n.) a mistake, blunder or indiscretion

fawn: (v.) to flatter or grovel, (v.) to seek notice or favor

fecundity: (n.) fruitfulness or fertility, the capacity of plentiful production

feign: (v.) to invent or represent fictitiously; (v.) to imitate deceptively

fete: (n.) a day of celebration or holiday; (n.) a festival

fiasco: (n.) a complete and utter failure

fiat: (n.) a capricious order or decree, an authoritative sanction

fiduciary: (n.) a person to whom property and/or property is entrusted

figment: (n.) something that is fabricated or made up

finesse: (n.) delicacy and/or refinement in performance; skillful and tactful diplomacy

finicky: (adj.) choosy, difficult to please

flaccid: (adj.) soft and limp; weak

flamboyant: (adj.) strikingly bold or showy, flashy; (adj.) ornate

fledgling: (n.) a newborn bird that recently acquired its feathers; (n.) an inexperienced person

fluctuation: (n.) continual change from one point to another, particularly related to a pitch or tone in one's voice

fluency: (n.) spoken or written with ease, particularly as related to a language; (adj.) easy and graceful; flowing

foible: (n.) a defect, flaw or weakness in a character

foist: (v.) to force another to accept especially by stealth or deceit

forbearance: (n.) tolerance in the face of challenge; (n.) patience

forte: (n.) a strong point or skill in which one excels; (n.) the stronger part of a sword blade

fortitude: (n.) mental and emotional strength in the face of challenge and adversity

fractious: (adj.) uncontrollable and/or unruly; (adj.) easily angered, irritable, quarrelsome

fraught: (adj.) filled with specific elements; (adj.) marked by or causing emotional distress

fritter: (v.) to squander away; (v.) to tear, break or cut into shreds

frolicsome: (adj.) full of fun; (adj.) in good spirits, playful

fructify: (v.) to make fruitful or productive; (v.) to bear fruit

frugality: (n.) economical in spending, frugal, requiring few resources

fulgent: (adj.) brightly shining; (adj.) dazzling

furor: (n.) an outburst of excitement or controversy; (n.) a prevailing fad or popular craze; (n.) rage, madness

furtive: (adj.) characterized by stealth; (adj.) expressive of concealed motives, purposes or intentions

G

gaff: (n.) harsh treatment or criticism

gambol: (n.) a playful skip or frolicking about

garbled: (v.) to confuse or distort to the point of that the result is misleading or incomprehensible

garrulous: (adj.) chatty and talkative

gazette: (adj.) a newspaper or official journal

geniality: (n.) having a friendly and pleasant disposition or manner

genre: (n.) a type or classification

genuflect: (v.) to tend one knee or touch one knee to the ground, in a sign or form of worship; (v.) to express a servile attitude

germane: (adj.) connected and relevant

gestate: (v.) to carry life from the point of conception to birth; (v.) to conceive and/or develop in the mind

gesticulation: (n.) a vigorous motion or gesture

glib: (adj.) lacking intellectual depth or capacity; (adj.) possessing only superficial plausibility; (adj.) persuasive in speech

gloaming: (n.) the time of day that immediately follows the sunset

glut: (v.) to fill (usually with food) beyond capacity; (v.) to flood (a market) with a plethora of goods to cause supply to exceed demand

glutinous: (adj.) having sticky and adhesive properties

goad: (n.) a long stick with a pointed end, used for prodding animals; (n.) a stimulus or means of urging

gorge: (n.) a deep ravine (usually with a river passing through it); to overeat

gourmand: (n.) a lover of food

gratuity: (n.) money paid which exceeds the amount due, such as in to a waitress or bellhop

H

hazardous: (adj.) risky; (adj.) dependent on chance

heinous: (adj.) atrocious, utterly reprehensible

heresy: (n.) an opinion or doctrine that is at odds with what is considered orthodox for a given situation or Institution, particularly in relation to religion

hierarchy: (n.) a system that involves ranking persons or groups of people above one another; (n.) an organized, governing body

hirsute: (adj.) covered with hair; (adj.) furry

hoodwink: (v.) to deceive or trick

holster: (n.) a leather or fabric case that is used for the purposes of holding a firearm in place; (n.) a case for carrying a small item

hortatory: (n.) urging toward a certain choice of behavior or action

hubbub: (n.) loud noise; (n.) confusion

humane: (n.) characterized by sympathy and caring for people; (adj.) relating to human studies

hummock: (n.) a hill or mound

hyperbole: (n.) an intentional exaggeration and/or embellishment regarding facts or circumstances; (n.) an overstatement

hypothecate: (v.) to pledge to a given creditor without offering any form of security, as in a mortgage

hypothetical: (adj.) speculative and theoretical in nature; unconfirmed

I

idiosyncrasy: (n.) a peculiarity or quirk in one's given disposition or behavior

ignominious: (adj.) humiliating

and/or embarrassing in nature; (adj.) reprehensible and disgraceful

illimitable: (adj.) characterized by an unlimited, unending nature

imbibe: (v.) to drink, swallow or absorb

imminent: (adj.) in the nature future, about to happen or occur

immutable: (adj.) not subject to change

impeach: (v.) to accuse or bring to court, particularly a public official; (v.) to question or call into account

impenitent: (adj.) without regret and unashamed

impervious: (adj.) not permitting of passage, impenetrable; (adj.) incapable of injury; (adj.) unmoved by persuasion

impious: (adj.) lacking reverence or respect; (adj.) irreverent

implacable: (adj.) unable to be pleased or mollified; (adj.) hard-hearted; (adj.) obdurate

imply: (v.) to suggest or refer

to something without explicitly stating it as such; (v.) to include as a necessary circumstance

importune: (v.) to demand by means of solicitation; (v.) to make unwanted advances or suggestions toward someone; (v.) to annoy

impotent: (adj.) lacking power or ability; (adj.) incapable; (adj.) lacking in physical strength

impromptu: (n.) a circumstance – particularly a speech – given without advanced preparation; (adj.) improvised

impropriety: (adj.) the quality of being improper or unsuitable; (adj.) an unseemly expression; (adj.) an incorrect use of a word or phrase; (adj.) rudeness; (adj.) misconduct

impunity: (n.) release from punishment or harm; (n.) mercy

imputation: (n.) a charge or accusation; (n.) an insinuation

inane: (adj.) lacking sense or sincere significance absurd; (adj.) immature

incessant: (adj.) continuing without interruption(s); (adj.) constant, ceaseless

incontinent: (adj.) uncontrolled and/or unrestrained, particularly in bodily function

incontrovertible: (adj.) not open for dispute or question; (adj.) irrefutable

incredulous: (adj.) skeptical and disbelieving; (adj.) dubious

inculcate: (v.) to instill by means of earnest and persistent repetition

indict: (v.) to officially charge or accuse, particularly in a court of law

inept: (adj.) unskilled and incompetent

inertia: (n.) inactivity- specifically in regards to motion

inference: (n.) a deduction or supposition about someone or something not arrived at through purely logical means

infraction: (n.) a violation or breech of a rule or contract

iniquitous: (adj.) characterized by wickedness and/or injustice; (adj.) sinful, immoral

innuendo: (n.) a subtle suggestion or implication

inordinate: (adj.) excessive and unwarranted; (adj.) overwhelming

insidious: (adj.) sinister and dangerous

intrepid: (adj.) courageous, fearless and brave

intrinsic: (adj.) essential to the nature of someone or something

inundate: (v.) to flood or overwhelm in an excessive manner

irreparable: (adj.) permanent (damage) beyond repair

iterate: (v.) to utter repeatedly, or in repetition

J

jaundiced: (adj.) affected with or colored by jaundice; (adj.) cynical, jaded; (adj.) full of prejudice

jejune: (adj.) unsophisticated and

sophomoric; (adj.) elementary

jeopardy: (n.) risk of death, loss, harm or injury; (n.) danger

jettison: (v.) to cast objects overboard in an effort to improve the stability of a moving object; (v.) to throw off something burdensome

jocose: (adj.) given to joking and humor

judicious: (adj.) using practical and proper judgment; demonstrating wisdom and/or good judgment

juncture: (n.) a critical point in time; (n.) a critical or urgent state of affairs, crisis

junta: (n.) a military-led government

K

ken: (n.) knowledge and understanding

kith: (n.) acquaintances or friends within the same vicinity

kleptomaniac: (n.) someone consumed by the impulsive need to steal, without economic motivation

L

lacerate: (v.) to slash or tear

laconic: (adj.)terse, brief, to the point, using few words

laggard: (n.) a straggler or one who lingers

languor: (n.) lack of energy; sluggishness; (n.) emotional sensitivity

lassitude: (n.) weariness, lack of energy, exhaustion

latent: (adj.) present but dormant and concealed

laudatory: (adj.) admiring; (adj.) expressing of praise

lewd: (adj.)inclined to lechery and/or vulgar behavior, obscene

liquidate: (v.) to break up; (v.) to pay a debt; (v.) to close a business; (v.) to exterminate or murder

lissome: (adj.) physiologically flexible; (adj.) agile

livid: (adj.) discolored; (adj.) very angry; (adj.) overcome with overwhelming emotion

lope: (v.) to sprint or scamper

lucent: (adj.) clear; semi-transparent; (adj.) transparent

lucid: (adj.) clear and cogent; (adj.) articulate and well-spoken; (adj.) rational, cool-headed

lugubrious: (adj.) characterized by sadness; (adj.) mournful, dismal

luminous: (adj.) radiating or reflecting light, shining; (adj.) brilliant

luster: (adj.) the state or quality of reflecting light, shine; (adj.) radiance of beauty

M

machinate: (v.) to contrive or plot; (v.) to conspire

malediction: (n.) a curse; (n.) the uttering of a curse

malefactor: (n.) a person who violates the law; (n.) reprobate

malignant: (adj.) evil and spiteful, showing ill-will and/or hatred towards others

malingerer: (v.) to feign illness, particularly in an effort to avoid duty or work

masticate: (v.) to chew; (v.) to reduce to a pulp by squashing or compressing

mediocre: (adj.) of moderate or ordinary quality

mellifluous: (adj.) smoothly flowing; (adj.) sweetened with honey

menial: (adj.) lowly and degrading, particularly in relation to work; (adj.) servile and submissive

mettle: (adj.) courage, fortitude

minion: (n.) a subordinate or underling

misgivings: (n.) doubts, uncertainties, reservations

mishap: (n.) an accident, calamity or disaster of an accidental nature

modish: (adj.) stylish, trendy

morbid: (adj.) implying an unhealthy state, attitude or interest in death; (adj.) gruesome, grisly

mordant: (adj.) caustic or sarcastic; (adj.) corrosive

morose: (adj.) melancholy, gloomy

mulct: (v.) to defraud or deprive someone of something

munificent: (adj.) characterized by generosity

mutable: (adj.) able to be adapted or changed; (adj.) capricious

myriad: (n.) an indefinite or unlimited number of person or things; (n.) ten thousand

N

nadir: (n.) a low point or "rock bottom, in terms of adversity or despair

nauseate: (v.) to sicken or disgust

nebulous: (adj.) vague and indefinable

necrology: (n.) a list of people who have died during a specified time period; (n.) an obituary

nemesis: (n.) a task a person is unable to conquer; (n.) an archenemy, opponent or rival; (n.) vengeance

neophyte: (n.) a novice or trainee; (n.) a person newly inducted into or converted into a faith or belief of a religious and/or spiritual nature

nicety: (n.) a delicate or fine point; (n.) a detail

noisome: (adj.) offensive or disgusting; (adj.) harmful

novice: (n.) a beginner or apprentice

noxious: (adj.) harmful or poisonous in nature; (adj. characterized by unpleasantness or offensiveness

numismatist: (adj.) a person who collects money, coin or metals

nurture: (v.) to feed and protect; (v.) to bring up, educate; (v.) to develop

O

obsequious: (adj.) characterized by a servile nature; (adj.)flattering, submissive

obsession: (n.) a fixation or passion

obstreperous: (adj.) hostile and bad-tempered

obtrude: (v.) to thrust forward upon a person; (v.) to project or stick out

occult: (adj.) of or pertaining to magic or astrology and involving secretive supernatural powers; (adj.) mysterious; hidden; (n.) supernatural affairs

odorous: (adj.) having a distinct odor; (adj.) scented

offal: (n.) the parts of a butchered animal considered inedible for human beings; (n.) rubbish, garbage

olfactory: (adj.) relating to the sense of smell

omniscient: (adj.) having complete and unlimited knowledge, awareness and understanding

omnivorous: (adj.) eating both animal and plant based foods

onus: (n.) a burdensome responsibility; burden of proof

opportunist: (n.) one who seized prospective opportunities; (n.) pioneer, trailblazer

opprobrious: (adj.) expressing of disdainful reproach; (adj.) conduct that yields disgrace or infamy

ostensible: (adj.) apparent and inconspicuous

P

pacify: (v.) to bring about or restore a peaceful state of mind; (v.) to appease; (v.) to subdue into submission, particularly by the use of military force

palliate: (v.) to relieve or lessen; (v.) to mitigate

paltry: (adj.) measly; (adj.) wretched

panacea: (n.) a remedy for all ailments, illnesses or disease; (n.) an answer or solution for all problems

panoply: (n.) a diverse range or display; (n.) a whole suit of armor; (n.) ceremonial attire

paradox: (n.) a statement or circumstance which seems intrinsically self-contradictory; (n.) any person thing or circumstance which displays an inherently contradictory nature

paragon: (n.) a model or archetype of excellence; (v.) to compare

pariah: (n.) an outcast; (n.) a person or animal that is overtly avoided

parsimonious: (adj.) excessively thrifty and economical; (adj.) cheap

pathos: (n.) that which invokes and arouses feelings of awe, pity or sorry; (n.) the feeling of pity and arousal

peculation: (n.) the fraudulent misuse of funds or property entrusted to you but not owned by you; (n.) embezzlement

pecuniary: (adj.) of or relating to money

penance: (n.) a punishment to

atone for a sin; an atonement

perfunctory: (adj.) performed out of routine or duty; (adj.) lacking genuine or sincere interest

perjury: (n.) the intentional giving of false statements while under sworn oath in a court of law

perspicacious: (adj.) having acute mental perception and understanding

pertinent: (adj.) relevant and applicable to a situation or set of circumstances

petrify: (v.) to frighten or terrify; (v.) to solidify or turn to stone

philanthropist: (n.) one who works to bring about the well-being of human kind through charitable donations and/or actions

phobia: (n.) a specific fear of an object or situation

pillage: (v.) to plunder and rob; (v.) to take in war as booty

pious: (adj.) devout in a religious sense; (adj.) self-righteous

piquant: (adj.) pungent and/or spicy in taste or flavor

placate: (v.) to appease or pacify someone

plebeian: (adj.) common, "blue-collar," working-class

pommel: (v.) to beat or strike; (n.) a knob on the hilt of a sword

posterity: (n.) future generations, a person's descendants

prattle: (v.) to idly chatter or babble

precipitate: (v.) to bring about, lead up to or hasten; (adj.) impulsive, rash

preponderance: (n.) a prevalence or predominance

prestige: (n.) esteemed status or standing; (n.) reputation

probe: (v.) to look into and investigate a situation or individual

probity: (n.) integrity and honor; (n.) decency

prodigal: (adj.) lavish and wasteful; (adj.) uncontrolled

promulgate: (v.) to make known, particularly one's opinions or theories; (v.) to publicize; (v.) to publicly teach a doctrine or creed

propensity: (n.) a tendency or inclination toward something; (n.) a predisposition

propound: (v.) to put forward or offer; (v.) to propose or promote

prototype: (n.) an example or mode; (n.) a trial product

provoke: (v.) to aggravate, incite or irritate; (v.) to cause or bring about

puerile: (adj.) childish and immature

pugnacious: (adj.) characterized by an aggressive and contentious nature

punctilious: (adj.) meticulous and scrupulous in nature; (adj.) socially correct and proper

purport: (v.) to assert, claim or declare; to imply or suggest; (n.) significance, importance

putrid: (adj.) in a state of decay or decomposition; (adj.) rotten; (adj.) rank

Q

quagmire: (n.) a situation or predicament from which disentanglement proves difficult; (n.) a swamp or marsh

quay: (n.) a dock or pier constructed along the edge of a body of water

queasy: (adj.) inclined to or experiencing nausea

quiescent: (adj.) at rest; (adj.) inactive

quietude: (n.) tranquility and stillness; (n.) peacefulness

quixotic: (adj.) idealistic in an unrealistic manner, (adj.) dreamy

R

ramification: (n.) a development, consequence or outcome that results from a problem

rancid: (adj.) sour, rotten

raucous: (adj.) harsh and strident; wild, (adj.) boisterous

ravage: (v.) to devastate and

destroy; (v.) to plunder and ransack

recapitulate: (v.) to repeat in a concise and succinct manner; (v.) to summarize or reiterate

recession: (n.) a depression or decline

reciprocate: (v.) to return or give back to

rectify: (v.) to correct, remedy and/or make right

reek: (v.) to stink or smell in a foul manner; to show signs of or suggest (n.) a foul stench or smell

refulgent: (adj.) brilliantly shining and/or gleaming

relinquish: (v.) to give up or actively surrender

remiss: (adj.) careless or negligent; (adj.) thoughtless

renunciation: (adj.) the act of turning away from, rejecting or denying

repository: (n.) a place in which things are safely kept; (n.) a warehouse; (n.) a tomb

reprisal: (n.) retaliation and/or an act of vengeance

reprobate: (n.) a degenerate; (n.) a depraved person

resplendent: (adj.) brilliantly shining and gleaming

retaliate: (v.) to revenge a wrong; (v.) to counterattack

revelry: (n.) festivities and celebrations; (n.) partying

reverberate: (v.) to echo, resound; (v.) to ring

rigor: (n.) strictness or severity in temperament or action

robust: (adj.) strong, healthy and hearty in physical condition

rococo: (adj.) ornate, decorative

ruddy: (adj.) reddish or rosy

rustic: (adj.) rural, country; pastoral

S

sacrilegious: (adj.) expressing of irreverence toward what is held sacred

sagacious: (adj.) showing keen discernment and exemplary judgment

salient: (adj.) prominent, markedly conspicuous

salubrious: (adj.) favorable to and fostering of body and/or mind health

salutary: (adj.) beneficial, constructive

sangfroid: (n.) coolness and composure, especially amidst trying and challenging circumstances

sanguine: (adj.) confident and optimistic, upbeat

sardonic: (adj.) characterized by a scornful and derisive attitude or nature

satiate: (v.) to supply in excess, (v.) to more than fully satisfy

scrupulous: (adj.) characterized by a conscientious and meticulous nature

seethe: (v.) to churn, boil; (v.) to fume or boil with rage; (v.) to teem, swarm

sequester: (v.) to remove or withdraw into solitude; (v.) to remove or separate

serrated: (adj.) possessing a jagged or saw-like edge

shoal: (n.) a place in which a body of water is shallow; any large number of people or things (v.) to cause to become shallow

simulate: (v.) to create a model, representation or recreation of

skeptic: (n.) one characterized by a cynical and doubting nature

skimp: (v.) to sparingly withhold

slander: (n.) defamation; words falsely spoken that damage someone's reputation

sloth: (n.) laziness and apathy, a disinclination toward work

slough: (n.) the out layer of the skin; (v.) to shed or cast off

smattering: (n.) a superficial knowledge of something

somatic: (adj.) of or related to the body, physical

sophomoric: (adj.) immature or overconfident and conceited

spate: (n.) a sudden outpouring or overwhelm

specious: (adj.) false, bogus

squalid: (adj.) unclean to the degree of filth; (adj.) seedy or immoral

squander: (v.) to waste or throw away

stalemate: (n.) a situation in which further action is obstructed and not possible

stigma: (n.) a mark or token of infamy; (n.) disgrace and dishonor

stipend: (n.) a periodic payment or schedule of fixed pay

stupor: (n.) a daze or state of unconsciousness

stymie: (v.) to present an obstacle, to stand in the way of

subversive: (adj.) undermining; dissident or rebellious, particularly against an established authority or government

succinct: (adj.) brief, concise and to the point

sully: (v.) to smear and dishonor; (v.) to pollute or contaminate

sumptuous: (adj.) luxurious and costly, (adj.) extravagant

supersede: (v.) to replace in power or authority; to surpass

surmise: (v.) to infer or guess without conclusive evidence

surreptitious: (adj.) sly, sneaky and covert

swathe: (v.) to wrap or enfold; (n.) a strip, ribbon or band

swelter: (v.) to suffer from excessive and overbearing heat

symmetry: (n.) balance and proportion

synchronous: (adj.) occurring at the same time, simultaneous

T

taciturn: (adj.) characterized by a reserved and quiet nature, uncommunicative

tactile: (adj.) tangible and concrete

tantalize: (v.) to torment and/or torture ; (v.) to excite or entice

tantamount: (adj.) equivalent in value and/or force

taut: (adj.) tight, rigid and staff; (adj.) tense, worried

tedium: (n.) the quality or state of being worrisome

temporal: (adj.) chronological and sequential; (adj.) earthly and secular

tenebrous: (adj.) dark or gloomy

tenet: (n.) an opinion, principle or doctrine

tepid: (adj.) lukewarm, halfhearted; moderate

terrestrial: (adj.) earthly and worldly

testy: (adj.) bad-tempered, crotchety, touchy

throes: (n.) a violent spasm or pain; (n.) a condition of agonizing struggle

timidity: (adj.) lacking in self-assurance or courage; (n.) nervousness and apprehensiveness

timorous: (adj.) fearful

titillate: (v.) to excite or arouse; (v.) to tickle by lightly stroking

tome: (v.) a book or volume

toxic: (adj.) of or relating to a poisonous and potentially lethal nature

translucent: (adj.) transparent; (adj.) easily understood

travail: (n.) a painfully difficult and burdensome work

trek: (v.) to make a slow and steady journey; (n.) a hike or walk

trepidation: (n.) fear, apprehension; disquiet

troth: (n.) faithfulness and fidelity; (n.) truth or verity

truncate: (adj.) terminating abruptly by having an end or cut off point; (v.) to approximate by ignoring all terms aside from an elect one; to shorten or abbreviate

turbid: (adj.) muddy due to sediment or foreign particles; (adj.) heavy, dark or dense; (adj.) in a state of turmoil

turpitude: (n.) vile and baseless depravity; (n.) a base act

U

ubiquitous: (adj.) existing or being everywhere at the same time; (adj.) omnipresent

umbrage: (n.) a feeling of anger, usually caused by offense; (n.) indignation

unanimity: (adj.) complete agreement and accord

uncanny: (adj.) unsettling in an eerie and mysterious way; (adj.) mysterious, creepy

unconscionable: (adj.) not restrained by good morals or scruples

unearth: (v.) to bring up out of the earth; (v.) to dig up

unfeigned: (adj.) sincere and genuine

ungainly: (adj.) ungraceful and awkward; (adj.) clumsy

unison: (adj.) in perfect accord

unseemly: (adj.) not in accordance with acceptable standards or good taste; (adj.) markedly improper

unsullied: (adj.) unblemished, untarnished, pure and immaculate

upbraid: (v.) to criticize or scold

usury: (n.) the lending or practice of money at exorbitant interest

V

vacuous: (adj.) lacking contents; (adj.) lacking in intelligence or capacity

vagary: (n.) an unexpected and/or unpredictable action or behavior

vapid: (adj.) lacking in life or flavor; (adj.) flat, dull

vegetate: (v.) to grow or sprout; (v.) to exist in a state of inactivity

vehement: (adj.) zealous and ardent; (adj.) strongly emotional

venerable: (adj.) deserving and worthy of respect by virtue of position, age, character or position; (adj.) worthy of reverence, within a religious context

verbose: (adj.) wordy and long-winded; (adj.) garrulous

versatile: (adj.) capable of and competent in multi-tasking or displaying of multi-talents; (adj.) varied, changeable

vestige: (n.) a trace, mark or indication; (n.) evidence

viable: (adj.) capable of life and development; (adj.) feasible and practical

victuals: (n.) food supplies (fit for human consumption)

vindictive: (adj.) malicious, bitter, mean or cruel

vitiate: (v.) to impair or reduce the quality of

vivacious: (adj.) lively and full of spiritedness

volition: (n.) the act of making a willful and conscious decision; (n.)

a conscious choice; (n.) the will

vouchsafe: (v.) to grant in a condescending method

W

wane: (v.) to decrease in strength or intensity; to draw to a close; (n.) a gradual decrease or decline; the waning of the moon

wanton: (adj.) willful and unprovoked; (adj.) immoral; (adj.) merciless; (adj.) excessively (adj.) unrestrained; (adj.) playful; (adj.) spoiled

welkin: (n.) sky

welter: (v.) to heave, roll or toss; to lie bathed in; (n.) a flurry or muddle

whorl: (v.) to spiral or twist

witticism: (n.) a witty remark or message

wraith: (n.) an apparition or phantom

wreak: (v.) to inflict vengeance upon a person; (v.) to punish; (v.)

to vent; (v.) to bring about

X

xenophobe: (n.) a person who is afraid of foreigners and their customs

Y

yank: (v.) to abruptly pull with a strong movement; (v.) to jerk

yelp: (v.) to utter a quick and sharp cry, as a result of pain

Z

zeal: (n.) passion for a person, cause or desire; (n.) fervor

zenith: (n.) a peak or summit; (n.) the highest point or station

Note: This list does not represent every vocabulary word that you will encounter on the GRE. Moreover, many words have more than one definition. In all cases in which I believe you will encounter a second, third, or even fourth definition of a word on the GRE, I have included it. Some words contained within this list have more definitions than listed here. In such cases, I have omitted additional definitions that I feel are extraneous to the GRE. Please note that you should consult several resources (books, dictionaries) to build your vocabulary for the GRE.

Although I am not usually the type to promote particular Web sites or resources, **http://supervocab.com** and **http://grelist.cgi** are truly useful to any GRE test taker. If you check this resource, you will quickly see how many words are out there for you to learn. It is a big world with a well-spring of words. Start learning them today.

READING COMPREHENSION PRACTICE QUESTION NUMBER ONE

To begin with, let's start with a somewhat brief passage. This will simply get you accustomed to reading a passage of information, attempting to apprehend the meaning as you read it and then answering questions about it afterwards. Remember, one of the best ways to improve your score on this section of the GRE is to do more reading on a consistent basis, then test how well you apprehend that knowledge afterwards.

- **Tip:** If you have already practiced several GRE sample questions and full-length tests prior to your test dates, you will not even need to spend your time reading directions on the test date. The directions never change. Familiarize yourself with them prior to your GRE.

Directions: The questions in this group are based on the content of the passage. After reading the passage, choose the best answer to each question. Answer each question based upon what is stated or implied in the passage.

Fats are a group of chemical compounds that contain fatty acids. We need fat in our diets to supply essential fatty acids (EFAs) — substances not produced by our bodies. A "chain" [straight line] of carbon atoms — studded by hydrogen atoms — comprises fatty acids.

(5)　　We find four fats in our diets: monounsaturated, polyunsaturated, saturated, and the dreaded trans. Mono- and polyunsaturated fats are by and large considered "good" fats and are present in foods like olives, avocados, and nuts. Foods high in polyunsaturated fats include sunflower oil, nuts, seeds, corn oil, and some fish. The two classes of polyunsaturated fatty acids (PUFAs) that we need are omega-3 and omega-6 fatty acids.

(10)   A saturated fatty acid has the maximum possible number of hydrogen atoms attached to each of its carbon atoms. Consequently, it is "saturated" with hydrogen atoms, unlike fatty acids that are "missing" one pair of hydrogen atoms in the middle of the molecule. Saturated fats — largely considered "bad" fats — mostly originate in foods from animals such as beef, beef fat, lamb, veal, pork, lard, poultry, butter, cream, milk, cheeses and other dairy products made from whole and two percent milk. Foods from plants that contain saturated fat include coconut, coconut oil, palm oil, and palm kernel oil, as well as cocoa butter.

(15)   Small amounts of trans fats can be found in animals and plants. The latest craze and health concern over trans fats, however, focuses on the trans fats created from the partial hydrogenation of vegetable oils. Partial hydrogenation is a process in which some of the missing hydrogen atoms are restored to polyunsaturated fats. The process fully converts liquid vegetable oil into a solid or semi-solid. Look for trans fats in processed foods — especially commercial baked products like cookies, cakes, crackers, and bread — as well as in cooking oils used for frying in restaurants. Trans fats keep Crisco solid at room temperature and also make cakes more moist, cookies softer, and increase the shelf life of many of these products. They take a licking, but keep on sticking!

1. The author suggests the following in the passage about types of fats (1-8)

    A. All fats are bad for one's health and should be avoided at all costs.

    B. Some fats are necessary for one's diet and should be included as part of a balanced, healthy nutrition plan.

    C. Saturated and trans fats are the only two types of fats that are safe for one to ingest.

D. There are various types of fats but determining which ones are safe or not safe is a difficult, if not impossible task.

E. All fats are healthy and one only needs to avoid any processed foods with "partially hydrogenated" in the list of ingredients.

2. The author's primary focus in this passage is to show:

A. Only mono and polyunsaturated fats are acceptable to ingest.

B. There are certain types of fats that we need in our diet.

C. Trans fats should be avoided because they involve the dangerous process of partial hydrogenation.

D. While trans fats can be found in processed foods, they are also found naturally in animals and plants and are therefore acceptable to include in one's diet.

E. Fats are dangerous and should be avoided in all forms.

3. The author's description of the foods in which trans fats can be found suggest which of the following conclusions (16-23):

A. It is impossible to avoid trans fats.

B. As long as the food item in question contains "good" fats in addition to "bad" or "trans" fats, the food in question is acceptable.

C. Consumers should check the labels and packages of any processed foods that they buy to see if they contain anything "partially hydrogenated."

D. Trans fats are found in plants and animals and processed foods but consumers should just avoid all processed foods.

E. Consumers should avoid the trans fats in both animals and plants.

4. It can be inferred from the passage that the most significant health problem that trans fats pose are:

A. They are saturated fats, which are the types of fats that are bad for our health.

B. They are most often found in non-plant food items.

C. They are naturally found in both plants and animals and therefore cannot be avoided.

D. They are unnaturally created from the partial hydrogenation of vegetable oils, which artificially restores some of the missing hydrogen atoms to the polyunsaturated fats.

E. All fats (including trans fats) should always be avoided.

ANSWER KEY:	
1. B	3. C
2. C	4. D

READING COMPREHENSION PRACTICE QUESTION NUMBER TWO

The questions in this group are based on the content of the passage. After reading the passage, choose the best answer to each question. Answer each question based upon what is stated or implied in the passage.

In his book, *Motivation and Personality*, Maslow theorizes about human needs according to a pyramid-based hierarchy. This hierarchy consists of five levels listed here in the successive order in which he formulates them: *Physiology, Safety, Love/Belonging, Esteem, and Self-Actualization.*

(5)   Maslow refers to needs on physiology, safety, love/belonging, and esteem levels as D-needs, or deficit needs. He reserves the label B-needs—being needs—for the self-actualization echelon.

(10)   According to Maslow, the satiation of one level of needs allows other (higher) needs to emerge, and then these, rather than the physiological hungers, dominate the organism. If the physiological needs are gratified, a new set of needs roughly categorized as "safety needs" (security, stability, dependency, protection, freedom from fear, anxiety, and chaos, need for structure, order, law, and limits, strength in the protectors, and so on) emerge. This process may progress through all the varying need levels.

(15)   According to Maslow, love level needs involve giving and receiving affection. Maslow asserts that little scientific information about the belongingness need exists, but that "we know in a general way the destructive effects on children of moving too often, of disorientation, of the general over-mobility that is forced by industrialization, of being without roots, or of despising one's roots, one's origins, one's group; of being torn from one's home and family, friends, and neighbors; of being a transient or a newcomer rather than a native." *(Motivation and Personality)*

(20).   Maslow divides esteem needs into two subsidiary sets: "first, the desire for strength, achievement, adequacy, mastery and competence, confidence in the face of the world, and independence and freedom; second, the desire for reputation or prestige, status, fame and glory, dominance, recognition, attention, importance, dignity and appreciation." (22)

(25)   Regarding self-actualization, Maslow states: "Even if all these needs are satisfied, we may still often (if not always) expect that a new discontent and restlessness will soon develop, unless the individual is doing what he or she, individually, is fitted for. Musicians must

make music, artists must paint, poets must write...What humans can be they must be...This need we may call self-actualization."

1. It can be inferred from the passage that Malsow theorizes about human needs according to a pyramid-like hierarchy, consisting of five levels:

    A. That are unrelated to each other.

    B. That are clearly related but by loose and ambiguous association.

    C. That are interdependent in that a higher level cannot be achieved until the needs on the lower level(s) has been satisfied.

    D. That go from ascending (physiological) to descending (self-actualization) in terms of importance.

    E. That can all be satisfied at one time.

2. The author's primary focus in this passage is to feature:

    A. How a human being can achieve self-actualization.

    B. How important even basic, physiological needs are.

    C. How ambiguous Maslow is about what love means to human beings.

    D. An overview of Maslow's theory concerning how human needs and motivation operate.

    E. An explanation of how a given individual can move from one level to the next in Maslow's pyramid/hierarchy of human needs.

3. The author's description of how one's progression from one need level to another works suggests the following conclusion:

A. The events one experiences over an entire lifetime will determine whether he or she advances from one level to the next.

B. If a given individual has not satisfied certain needs on a given need level, they cannot possibly advance to the next level and its set and/or subset of needs.

C. If a given individual satisfies needs on one of the lowest levels, like the physiology and love/belonging levels, he or she can achieve self-actualization so long as he or she discovers what he or she has been born to do in this life.

D. Anyone, regardless of circumstances or events, can advance and progress through all of the levels in the pyramid/hierarchy of human needs.

E. Peoples' physiology level needs are the least related to their self-actualization level needs.

4. The author infers that the following most clearly relates to the achievement of a human being's self-actualization:

A. The reduction of restlessness through attempting new activities.

B. Doing what one is most fitted to do.

C. Advancing through all the levels of the pyramid of human needs.

D. Achieving the highest success in one's career.

E. Satisfying one's physiological needs in order to progress upward through the hierarchy.

ANSWER KEY:	
1. C	3. B
2. D	4. B

READING COMPREHENSION PRACTICE QUESTION NUMBER THREE

The questions in this group are based on the content of the passage. After reading the passage, choose the best answer to each question. Answer each question based upon what is stated or implied in the passage.

The traditional date of Lao Tzu's birth is recognized as 604 B.C., although this date as well as his historical existence is still debated by modern historical scholars. While Lao Tzu is recognized as a philosopher, 'religious' Taoism emerged from his philosophies several centuries later. Chuang Tzu and Liehzi are recognized as the two other most important figures of Taoism, and like Lao Tzu, they are also viewed as philosophical figures. It is important to note that when these individuals wrote texts and developed theories, they were not trying to start a religion. The students and followers of these figures bear the responsibility for the religion of Taoism that started some years later.

(5)   Tao is understood to mean "the Way," but not in the sense that the Western mind would think of "way" (shall we go this way or that way, for instance). In Taoism, the Tao or "way" is immanent in everything. It is a pantheistic religion, so everything is viewed as Divine; there are no gods that reside outside the world and separate from us. The term "pantheism" comes from a Greek word that means "everything." As Chuang Tzu says in *The Inner Chapters*, the Tao is in everything; there is nothing that does not house the Tao.

In Taoism, everything is One, connected, and in unity. The Tao itself is empty; it is a force or motion that unifies. Chuang Tzu uses the metaphor of the hub of a wheel to explain this seemingly paradoxical concept. To understand this, we must think of older wagon wheels, in which the spokes point toward the hub—which is hollow and empty but which makes the wheel useful. The hub itself is empty and without content; it serves rather as functionality.

This essence of functionality is the Tao. It emanates from and binds everything together. It is pliant, but very strong. Because it unifies, it naturally promotes life, growth, and evolution.

It can be inferred from the passage that Lao Tzu:

A. Intended to start the religion of Taoism and was successful.

B. Is the founder of Taoism.

C. Is the fonder of both the philosophical and religious Taoist movements.

D. Had some philosophical theories that scholars now label "Taoist," but never intended to start a religious movement.

E. Was pantheistic and started Taoism, since Hinduism was already popular in other parts of the world.

2. The author's primary focus in this passage is to:

A. Explain what "Taoism" is.

B. Identify and abolish misconceptions about "Taoism."

C. Compare Taoism to other pantheistic religions.

D. Liken Taoist principles to the spokes of a wheel, thereby invoking the use of a metaphor.

E. Show how the meaning and philosophies of Taoism are vague and esoteric.

3. The author's differentiation between philosophical and religious Taoism serves to:

A. Show the reader that there is a difference between the two.

B. Show the reader that what began as philosophical theory evolved into a religious tradition—through no intention of Lao Tzu.

C. Show the reader the differences between the philosophical and religious precepts of Taoism.

D. Show the reader that no clear distinction between the philosophical and religious aspects of Taoism exist.

E. Show the reader that Taoism is both a philosophy and a religion.

ANSWER KEY:

1. C   2. B   3. B

READING COMPREHENSION PRACTICE QUESTION NUMBER FOUR

The questions in this group are based on the content of the passage. After reading the passage, choose the best answer to each question. Answer each question based upon what is stated or implied in the passage.

Scholars of philosophy and laymen alike commonly view "motivation" as what drives an individual to perform a certain action. Phrases such as "Police Search for Motive" regularly appear in print media or online headlines worldwide. However, the quest to understand this subject readily exists outside the criminal sphere.

(5)   Lascaux, a complex of caves in southwestern France, contains some of the earliest known art—dating back to somewhere between 13,000 and 15,000 BC, perhaps as far back as 25,000 BC. Philosophers, anthropologists, and other historians continue to speculate on the motivations for the cave paintings. Some scholars maintain that humans are "social animals," and these scholars suggest that the Lascaux cave art signifies the expression of humanity's social aspect. Others, such as Henri Édouard Prosper Breuil — a French archaeologist, anthropologist, ethnologist, and geologist — interpret the paintings as "hunting magic" intended to increase the number of animals within close proximity.

(10)   Another theory, more modern in origin, interprets the art as the work of Cro-Magnon shamans. According to this perspective, shamans retreated into the caves, entered into a trance state, and then painted images of their visions. A desire to draw power from the caves' walls might account for the Shamans' motivations; we do not know this for certain.

(15)   As a result of the curiosity we perpetually demonstrate in understanding what propels our actions, philosophers and psychologists have consistently sought to formulate paradigms, models, and explanations for motivation. What is motivation? Does motivation exist within us, outside us, or is it a synergistic process between self and environment?

1. It can be inferred from the above passage that: (10-16)

    A. Cro-Magnons painted in the caves of Lascaux, France to draw power from the caves' walls.

B. We do not know assuredly know the motivations for why Cro-Magnons painted in the caves of Lascaux, France.

C. Cro-Magnons painted in the Lascaux caves because they were social animals.

D. Cro-Magnons were motivated to paint in the Lascaux caves in an attempt to invoke "hunting magic."

E. The desire to enter trance-like states motivated the famous Lascaux cave paintings.

2. The author's primary focus in this passage is to show:

A. Various theories seek to explain "motivation," whether the explanations are retrospective (as in the case of the Lascaux cave paintings) or current (scholars of philosophy, laymen, police).

B. Various theories exist which try to elucidate "motivation" and that the most popular theories are those pronounced by scholars of philosophy.

C. Various "motivation" theories exist, but theories more modern in origin provide better explanations than other theories.

D. So many theories which seek to explain "motivation" exist that the subject is not worth investigating.

E. All "motivation" theories are equal.

ANSWER KEY:	
1. B	2. A

READING COMPREHENSION PRACTICE QUESTION NUMBER FIVE

The questions in this group are based on the content of the passage. After reading the passage, choose the best answer to each question. Answer each question based upon what is stated or implied in the passage.

A recurring question we receive at the Utah Geological Survey is: "Where can I get colloidal mineral supplements?" This article does not address where to purchase them, but what these products are and where they come from. "Colloidal mineral supplements" are cloudy liquids marketed as dietary supplements under many product names.

(5)   Suppliers claim that they provide minerals not available from today's foods. To a believer in alternative medicine, these panaceas are touted to have the power to greatly improve your health by providing numerous essential minerals. To a skeptic, they are nothing more than snake oil sold to unwary fools.

(10)   As a geologist, not a doctor, I am unsuited to comment on positive, negative, or non-existent potential health effects. What I can address is the geology of the rocks used to produce these products in Utah.

(15)   Soaking specific types of pulverized shale in water allows some of the shale's organic matter to dissolve, creating a liquid that is termed a shale leachate. Colloidal mineral supplements are nothing more than shale leachates. Fine particles, which do not dissolve, are also suspended in these leachates.

(20)   At least some, if not all, of these elixirs are water-leached from carbonaceous shales mined from the Emery coalfield of Emery County in central Utah (more specifically the "G" bed / middle coal zone of the Ferron Sandstone Member of the Mancos Shale).

The Ferron Sandstone was deposited approximately 90 million years ago during the Late Cretaceous, near the close of the age of dinosaurs.

(25)   Within a coalfield, individual zones and beds vary in their ratio of carbonaceous material (altered plant material) to sediment (clay, silt, and sand). Carbonaceous shales are interbedded with purer coal, but contain much more inorganic silt than coal and are thus not useful as a fuel. However, the organic matter in these shales is essentially the same as the organic matter that composes purer coal.

(30)   The organic matter in the shales and coals originated as plant material that accumulated in wetlands and bogs. The organic matter began to change to peat when bacteria broke down the plant material. The peat was then buried by sediment and more plant material, which raised the temperature and pressure. As the peat compressed, water, carbon dioxide, and methane gas were forced out. With increasing heat and pressure the peat was converted to the types of organic matter found in coals and carbonaceous shales. After a great length of time, uplift and erosion exposed the coalfields so they can be mined at or near the surface.

(35)   At the surface, weathering further alters the carbonaceous shales before they are mined. After being mined, the carbonaceous shale is crushed and then soaked in water. After a period of time, perhaps three to four weeks, the water (leachate) is filtered off, bottled, and marketed as a "colloidal mineral supplement."

© 2008, Mark Milligan, Utah Geological Survey

1. It can be inferred from the passage that: (1-4)

    A. The author has a clear opinion about whether colloidal mineral supplements should be marketed and sold or not.

B. The author has an opinion about whether colloidal mineral supplements should be marketed or sold but does not want to sway the reader one way or the other.

C. The author has an opinion about whether colloidal mineral supplements should be marketed, and intends to focus his article on that opinion.

D. The author may or may not have an opinion about whether colloidal mineral supplements should be marketed and sold, but intends to focus his article on their origins.

E. The author does not have an opinion on whether colloidal mineral supplements should be marketed and sold.

2. The author posits a disclaimer in the article for the purposes of: (9-11)

A. Confusing the reader.

B. Explicitly stating his expertise on the subject matter and clearly delineating what he can because he cannot elucidate about colloidal minerals and colloidal mineral supplements for the reader.

C. Comparing himself with a doctor and showing that he has more knowledge about the subject of colloidal minerals and colloidal mineral supplements.

D. Distancing himself from any debate about whether colloidal mineral supplements should be marketed and sold.

E. Both B and D.

3. The author implies the following about colloidal mineral supplements in the conclusion of his article:

A. Colloidal mineral supplements should not be marketed or sold.

B. Colloidal mineral supplements should be marketed and sold.

C. There is no proper means by which to determine whether colloidal minerals should be marketed and sold.

D. The origins of colloidal minerals are rather organic and ordinary in nature and the bottling of "colloidal mineral supplements" is suggestive in nature and implies more than the origins point to.

E. No relationship between the origins of colloidal minerals and the current colloidal mineral supplements on the market today exist.

ANSWER KEY:		
1.D	2. B	3. D

Go to **www.ets.org** for more practice questions.

ANALOGY PRACTICE QUESTIONS

1. DENT : DESTROY

    A. weep : laugh

    B. curl : roll

    C. river : tributary

    D. drip : gush

    E. bend : angle

2. CHEW : MOUTH

    A. dress : sleeve

    B. walk : legs

    C. grind : axe

    D. read : book

    E. solve : equation

3. LIBERATE : CONFINE

    A. open : book

    B. enfranchise : enslave

    C. appease : pacify

    D. mollify : conciliate

    E. reject : omit

4. FLOURISH : FADE

    A. assist : aid

    B. redundant : repetitive

    C. entice : repel

    D. add : divide

    E. proliferate : grow

5. ALGEBRA : MATHEMATICS

- A. English : grammar
- B. ontology : philosophy
- C. feminist : feminism
- D. science : biology
- E. history : geology

6. ACUMEN : INSIGHT

- A. evanescent : vanishing
- B. malevolence : kindness
- C. occlusion : passage
- D. hedonism : asceticism
- E. impunity : punishment

7. MITIGATE : MODERATE

- A. punish : forgive
- B. speculate : assert
- C. rescind : repeal
- D. bolster : destroy
- E. burgeon : grow

8. LAZY: SHIRK

- A. angry : placate
- B. rancorous : appease
- C. recalcitrant : submit
- D. despiteful : challenge
- E. clumsy : botch

9. MINCE : EMPHASIZE

- A. rail : praise
- B. enervate : restore
- C. accentuate : stress
- D. quibble : agree
- E. vandalize : damage

10. VINDICTIVE : SPITE

- A. hospitable : courtesy
- B. infamous : honor
- C. lazy : haste
- D. thrifty : waste
- E. despondent : glee

ANSWER KEY:	
1. D	6. A
2. B	7. C
3. B	8. E
4. C	9. D
5. B	10. A

Go to **www.ets.org** for more practice questions.

SENTENCE COMPLETION PRACTICE QUESTIONS

1. Hamlet, in the famous play by William Shakespeare, was known for his _____ disposition; Shakespeare never depicted him as a gleeful or jubilant individual.

    A. melancholic

    B. cheerful

    C. singular

    D. chauvinistic

    E. fastidious

2. Any avid business man or woman in today's world must constantly broaden his or her horizons; a(n) _____ attitude does one a distinct disservice in our current age of ever-changing communication and technology.

    A. yielding

    B. appeasing

    C. submissive

    D. rigid

    E. diverse

3. My CD collection at home features a wide array of CDs from various genres, thereby reflecting my _____ musical palette.

    A. narrow

    B. diaphanous

    C. eclectic

    D. futile

    E. redundant

4. Fast food restaurants are a(n) _____ symbol of our current consumer oriented society; one can find a multitude of them on virtually every city street corner.

    A. iconic
    B. ubiquitous
    C. covert
    D. occlusive
    E. bombastic

5. Psychologists need to _____ their arguments with relevant data, otherwise, their theories only serve as mere _____.

    A. test - information
    B. prove - assertions
    C. refine - hypotheses
    D. buttress - speculations
    E. promulgate - conjectures

6. The work of the artist Salvador Dali may be deemed by some as _____, yet he remains hailed as a(n) _____ artist by art historians and patrons of the arts alike.

    A. morbid - defunct
    B. superficial - praised
    C. eccentric - criticized
    D. jubilant - lauded
    E. morose - respected

7. Aboriginal societies are often criticized for what some may view as their _____ living conditions, which sharply contrast the contemporary and technologically advanced environment of the majority of the global world at large.

    A. occult
    B. uncivilized
    C. obtuse
    D. educated
    E. questionable

ANSWER KEY:	
1. A	5. A
2. D	6. E
3. C	7. B
4. A	

ANTONYM PRACTICE QUESTIONS

1. AUSPICIOUS

    A. unfortunate
    B. functional
    C. teleological
    D. bombastic
    E. persuasive

2. DILETTANTISH

    A. amateurish
    B. insincere
    C. refined
    D. professional
    E. good-natured

3. RAIL

    A. complain
    B. praise
    C. decry
    D. disparage
    E. rant

4. HOSPITABLE

    A. intimate
    B. oblique
    C. rude
    D. unofficial
    E. good-natured

5. EXUBERANT

    A. dim
    B. eccentric
    C. lumbered
    D. pied
    E. lively

6. RECALCITRANT

    A. unrefined
    B. obsequious
    C. cooperative
    D. enticing
    E. quotidian

7. RECTIFY

    A. promulgate
    B. damage
    C. rail
    D. qualify
    E. mince

8. AUGMENT

    A. minimize
    B. decorate
    C. pine
    D. grouse
    E. enlist

ANSWER KEY:	
1. A	5. E
2. D	6. C
3. B	7. B
4. C	8. A

NEW QUESTION TYPE: TEXT COMPLETION

Beginning in November of 2007, ETS introduced a new type of verbal test question called "Text Completion." At the time that this book is being written, ETS is still in the process of testing these questions. Since ETS has not yet officially released this question type as one that will count toward an individual's score, it is currently inappropriate for me to offer "sample" questions, as ETS may tweak this question type before officially releasing it.

You should know the following about this new type of question:

- Passages are one to five sentences in length.

- Each question contains two to three blanks.

- There are three answer choices per blank.

- The answer choices for each blank function independently. If you fill in one blank incorrectly, this will not affect your score on another blank.

- As with other ETS questions, no partial credit is given. Each blank is either "correct" or "incorrect."

All strategies and practice questions for this type of question are still owned by ETS. You are encouraged to visit **www.ets.org** immediately to learn more about this type of question. At the time of this publication, ETS currently provides an online bulletin with a few brief strategies and a few sample questions.

CHAPTER 9 HOMEWORK

1. Decide how you wish to break down the comprehensive vocabulary list in this book. Do you want to study A–D a certain day of the week, E–H another day, and so on? Conversely, you could work on the list backward, just to shake things up. Whatever you decide, make a plan. Put this on your study schedule every day, at least six days a week. To study for vocabulary, you should:

- Carefully read over the words, definitions, and synonyms.

- Write out the words and definitions on sheets of paper.

- Write out the words and definitions on flashcards. Then, carry the flashcards around with you so that you can study in your spare time.

- Purchase vocabulary flashcards as a complement to the comprehensive vocabulary list in this book.

2. Schedule when you will practice sentence completions, analogies, antonyms, reading comprehension, and entire verbal reasoning tests. Remember to pace yourself. Start gradually by studying and practicing the individual sections first. Work your way up to doing entire test sittings at once.

3. Keep *practicing, practicing,* and *practicing* more. *You cannot practice enough.* After you do the practice questions in this book, log onto **www.ets.com** for more practice questions and answers. Also, when you register for the GRE, they will send you a software packet that includes practice tests. Utilize those! You can also go to the bookstore and purchase every prep book on the market for the simple purposes of using the CDs in them (which contain more practice tests).

CHAPTER 10

How to Prepare for the Quantitative Section of the GRE

MATH ABILITY: "THE SKINNY"

- The math (quantitative section) consists of 30 questions on the paper-based test, or 28 questions on the computer-based test.

- The types of questions you will be tested on are quantitative comparison questions, quantitative questions (standard multiple-choice questions), and data interpretation questions.

- How well you perform on this section hinges on your knowledge of mathematics and your ability to keep cool, think clearly, and read questions carefully. ETS® and most GRE prep books claim that the skills required to score well on this section range between elementary and high school level mathematics skills. Review the basic mathematical concepts in this book and through the ETS® software. If you find yourself experiencing difficulty in answering the questions, you just need to study and practice more. It sounds simple. Math, though, can be learned.

- The amount of time you spend on each question will depend on how well you can answer that type of question. If the question involves algebra and algebra is your weakness, you may take longer to answer this type of question. As a past GRE test-taker, I have found that the data interpretation questions take the longest to answer. You cannot quickly scan the graph and answer the questions correctly. You must read the questions very carefully and then skillfully answer them.

- As with the verbal section of the GRE, do not spend an excessive amount of time attempting to answer questions that you simply do not know how to answer. If you are presented with a question that you do not know how to answer, there is no need to waste time on the question. Also – although I hate to be the bearer of bad news – there are no tips and strategies that can help you circumvent this type of situation. If you have a reasonable idea of how to answer question, you will learn tips and strategies in this section to help you confirm your answer. If the question produces nothing but a blank stare from you, give it your best guess, or guess "C" (the third choice), which is the most commonly guessed correct answer.

Here is the breakdown of the math section:

- 14 quantitative comparison questions

- 10 "discrete" quantitative questions (multiple-choice questions)

- 4 data interpretation questions

- New Question Type (Possible): Numeric Entry

Like the verbal reasoning section, ETS® and GRE prep books state that the quantitative section of the GRE tests skills accumulated over a long time. One difference with this section, though, is that ETS® does emphasize high school as the period during which one would have acquired these mathematical skills. I think if the skills required to perform well on this section of the GRE are acquired in high school math, we should be seeing perfect or near perfect scores from several GRE test-takers, particularly those who have just finished their undergraduate degree. Since math — whether algebra, geometry or otherwise — is built into college curriculum, college students continue to use those skills. In such a case, they should do well on this portion of the GRE.

Such is not the case, however. Many students find this section of the test extremely challenging. Of course, depending on what field a given student is in, he or she may find it to be the easiest portion. Either way you slice it, though, everyone must study for this portion of the GRE. The reason that everyone must study for this section of the test is because no GRE test taker took their high school math classes yesterday, or last month for that matter. Have you ever heard the expression, "Use it or lose it?" This is often the case with math — particularly when rules and formulas are involved. Furthermore, this is a standardized test with intricately designed problems. In high school math class, you were given simpler questions to answer on your test. Also, your test was not multiple choice, with incorrect answer choices sprinkled in with the correct one. Finally, you did not take your high school math test after writing for one hour and fifteen minutes straight. Also, in high school, you might have been able to jot down some formulas you wanted to remember on some scratch paper before your test started. When you take the GRE, you will not be allowed to jot anything down on scratch paper before your test starts. If you do, you will be removed from the testing center.

For those with math anxiety, this may all sound somewhat discouraging, but do not despair. No one should treat this section of the GRE any less seriously than any other section of the GRE. You should study just as hard. You should learn what you need to learn. In this case, you need to know your formulas and the "how to's" for solving certain equations. You also need to remember certain rules that apply in the mathematical world. This is no different — and should not be more or less stressful — than learning your vocabulary, brushing up on your reading comprehension skills, and dusting off your pen or pencil to work on your writing techniques. As with every other section of the GRE, if you forget about the scoring system and what you are going to do if you do not know how to answer a question and instead concentrate on relearning the maze of mathematical ins and outs, you will perform with excellence on this portion of the test.

Remember, much like learning the English language, math consists of building blocks. Concentrate on relearning basic arithmetic skills first, even if you do not find that necessary. Also, at this point in your test preparation journey, you should start doing any possible math by hand instead of using a calculator. Then, go to the next "building block." Review algebra. Memorize your formulas. Relearn how to solve algebraic equations. Next, tackle geometry. Remember, just because funny looking shapes with formidable sounding names like "parallelograms" are now involved, it does not mean that you have stepped outside the mathematical world. You must now simply learn to apply your skills in a new and different way — to shapes, instead of formulas. Last, you should brush up on your data analysis skills. Do not make the mistake I did on my first go-around with the GRE. Do not skip working on the data analysis section. I know what you are thinking: "I know how to read a graph; why should I waste my time looking at graphs?" Trust me, you may know how to look at a graph, but you will also need to know how to interpret one. Moreover, some of the data analysis questions will involve some amount of computation and critical thinking skills, so be prepared.

As with the verbal reasoning and analytical writing sections of the GRE, remember *there is no substitute for practice on the quantitative section.* Sure, you can memorize all of the formulas and work over a few problems, but if you do not consistently practice answering these questions over and over again, you will not do well on this section of the GRE. At the risk of sounding repetitive, I am compelled to remind you once again: The GRE is a timed test taken under stressful conditions. Your goal is to run on auto-pilot the day of the test. You do not want to be scratching your head and asking yourself, "How do I calculate the circumference of a circle again?" While you may eventually remember and figure it out, just think how much easier this would be if you had just practiced that type of problem fifteen times before the test. You would answer the question in less than ten seconds.

Many people have difficulty with the math section of the test, particularly since it requires you to *apply* your mathematics skills. In that respect, this section is unlike the verbal section. The verbal section, as I mentioned earlier, is essentially a vocabulary test. Therefore, if you learn several vocabulary words and practice using them before the test, you are very likely to increase your score on this section of the GRE. Math, though, is different. You cannot just memorize several math formulas and expect to walk into the testing center and do well. Mathematics requires that you know *what to do* with a particular formula. It also demands that you know *how to apply* the particular knowledge at hand. In that respect, the verbal section is easier; you are already given the structure of how to apply your vocabulary knowledge: You find opposites of words for antonyms, similar comparisons of words for analogies, appropriate choices for sentence completion questions, and read carefully for reading comprehension.

While studying and learning math formulas and practicing the application of those formulas can help you increase your GRE score, this book cannot teach you all of the math that you should have learned in high school. So, do not let this cause you anxiety. If, however, you find yourself having trouble, consider hiring a tutor.

Remember, many of the prep books on the market are over 500 pages long. This does not necessarily mean that these books will help you increase your score. It does mean, however, that none of those books, nor this book, alone can help you learn everything you should have learned in high school math. Hire a tutor now if you have trouble with math and need to score high on this section of the GRE.

> ## Tip #60: Back to basics — brush up on your basic arithmetic skills.

The quantitative section of the GRE does not feature specific questions that solely test your arithmetic skills. Rather, it will assume that you already have these "building blocks" under your belt, so to speak. You will not get questions like this on the GRE:

"What is an integer?"

"How do you convert a percentage into a fraction?"

Rather, the GRE will assume that you already have the basic arithmetic skills required to answer questions of a less simple nature. This news should not scare you, but excite you. For those of you who vaguely remember high school math and performed reasonably well in college level math courses, we are simply going to rebuild your mathematical knowledge, starting with the basic building blocks of arithmetic. Anyone who did not do well in high school or college math gets good news as well: You just have to build instead of rebuild your knowledge. Trust me, it *can* be done. I struggled in high school math, performed at an average level in college mathematics, and managed to raise my quantitative section score of the GRE by several points, just by studying on my own. I did not get a tutor. I did not take a prep course. I just worked hard, studied and practiced.

Here are the following arithmetic concepts that you will want to familiarize yourself with for this section of the GRE (Remember, this is a cursory review and a basic handle on mathematical skills is assumed of any GRE test taker):

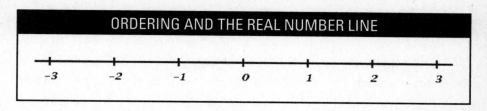

ORDERING AND THE REAL NUMBER LINE

"Real Numbers" are just that — numbers that we humans have designated as real. They are also referred to as "integers" (see below). We identify the numbers which comprise all real numbers as "the real number system." Therefore, the "Real Number Line" is simply a visual representation of the real number system. It is what the math looks like, in other words. The real number line appears as a horizontal line that extends from a "point of origin" (0) and extends in both directions (both positive and negative) towards "infinity."

More important, the real number line is associated with what we call a "unit of length." A given positive number corresponds to a point a unit away from the origin (0) on the right, and a negative number corresponds to a point on the line a unit away from the origin on the left. This is illustrated in the figure above.

- **Tip:** Notice that regardless of whether a given number corresponds to a point on the line that is either positive or negative (a or –a), the unit of length is always positive.

Moreover, also related to this concept, we can use the number line to represent the mathematical concept that a number x **is greater than** a number y in symbols

$$x > y$$

assuming that on the real number line (see above), x appears to the right of y.

INTEGERS

All whole, counting numbers, such as -1, 0, 1, 2, and 3 are integers. On the above real number line, all whole numbers are integers. More important than the obvious definition of an integer are the rules for performing arithmetic operations when you use them. Here is a quick review of a few rules you will want to remember for your GRE:

- Whenever you multiply an integer by 0, the answer is always 0.

- Whenever you multiply or divide two integers with different signs (positive and negative), the answer will always yield a negative integer.

- Whenever you multiply or divide two negative integers, the answer always yields a positive integer. I know that this point seems ironic, but it is true.

- Whenever you multiply two integers, the answer yields a third integer. The two integers you multiplied together are called *factors*. The answer is the *product*. The product is always a *multiple* of both factors, and is therefore also *divisible* by both factors (as long as the factors are not equal to zero).

- Whenever an integer x is divisible by an integer y, it is true that y is a *divisor or factor of x*.

- In the set of positive integers (all whole, counting numbers above zero with no fractions or decimals) any integer that has only two positive divisors is called a *prime number*.

- For example, the first six prime numbers are 2, 3, 5, 7, 11, and 13.

Again, think in terms of building blocks. When you take the practice questions at the end of the chapter, you will understand the meaning of this. You are not going to see a GRE test question that asks, "What are the first three prime numbers?" ETS® will not present you with a question like, "What is the definition of a divisor?" Therefore, while it is important to review and remind yourself of these basic building blocks, memorizing them will not help you achieve a higher GRE score. If memorization makes you feel comfortable and you want to look up and memorize every prime number, go ahead. However, you are likely better off spending your time answering practice questions that involve integers, roots and exponents. Remember, this is a multiple choice test that involves calculations. You will not be asked for definitions or lists. Also, if at any point you feel that you need more clarification about any topic, you can go to your school or local library and check out a mathematical textbook. You can also use the ETS® review bulletins, provided through their Web site.

ABSOLUTE VALUE

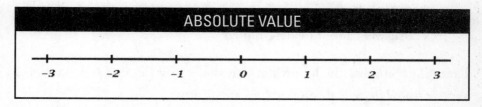

Remember the real number line? On the GRE, you may see a question about "Absolute Value." The mathematical symbol used to refer to absolute value looks like this:

$$|x|$$

The absolute value of a real number is simply its distance from the origin. The rules of absolute value are not the same as unit of length, though. As you recall from above, the unit of length of a or b is the number of units of length a or b are away from the number line, regardless of whether a or b are positive or negative.

- **Tip:** The absolute value will always be positive. If x is positive, then the absolute value of x is positive. If x is negative, the absolute value is positive. This looks as follows:

$$|x| = x \qquad |-x| = x$$

Absolute value answers the question of how far an integer is from the point of origin (0) on the real number line. It does not address the question of which direction on the number line the integer is placed.

Example: Simplify the following:

$|-4|$

    a. 0
    b. -4
    c. 4
    d. 16
    e. Answer cannot be determined

Example: Simplify the following: C is the answer because it is positive 4 and we know that all absolute values are positive.

$|3 - 8|$

    a. $|-5|$
    b. $|-8|$
    c. $|0|$
    d. $|3|$
    e. Answer cannot be determined

To simplify this problem, first determine the value of 3 − 8. Since you know that the larger number is negative, you also know that the answer will be negative. 3 − 8 is -5. Therefore, the question can be simplified as such:

$|-5|$

The absolute value of $|-5|$ is 5.

FRACTIONS

A fraction is simply shorthand for division. Fractions can be written in two forms, as long as in both the following cases, the numerator (*a*) and denominator (*b*) are whole numbers and the denominator is not equal to 0:

$$\frac{a}{b} \qquad \text{or} \qquad a/b$$

A number that can be described as a ratio or fraction is a rational number. Since fractions are simply shorthand for division, the above fractions are simply shorthand for *a* divided by *b*. On the GRE, you will see the first form of fractions most frequently.

Remember, the GRE is a test of how to do high school math. It is also multiple choice. Therefore, the GRE will not ask you for the definition of a fraction. You will, though, need to apply your knowledge of how to work with fractions. You should, therefore, familiarize yourself with the rules of fractions:

- To add two fractions with the same denominator, add the numerators and place the sum over the denominator, because the denominator stays the same.

- If the denominators are not the same: 1.) Find the least common denominator; 2.) Write the equivalent fractions using this denominator; 3.) Add the fractions. Reduce for a final answer that correlates with one of the multiple choice answers, if necessary.

Example: Identify the value of the following:

$$\frac{3}{4} + \frac{1}{8}$$

a. $\dfrac{4}{32}$

b. $\dfrac{4}{8}$

c. $\dfrac{7}{8}$

d. $\dfrac{4}{4}$

e. Answer cannot be determined.

In this example problem, the least common denominator is 8.

$$\dfrac{3}{4} = \dfrac{6}{8} \text{ and } \dfrac{1}{8} = \dfrac{1}{8}. \quad \dfrac{6}{8} + \dfrac{1}{8} = \dfrac{7}{8}.$$

Therefore, the third answer choice is correct.

- To multiply two fractions, multiply the two numerators and multiply the two denominators (the denominators need not be the same).

- To divide one fraction by another, first invert the fraction you are dividing by, and then proceed as you would in multiplication.

- To reduce fractions, express the numerator and denominator as the products of their factors. Then, cancel any factors that are common to both the numerator and denominator, or find the greatest common divisor (GCD) and divide both the numerator and denominator by that number. In this case, "divisor" means the greatest integer that can be divided into the number without leaving a remainder.

Example: Simplify:

$$\frac{6}{8}$$

    a. $\dfrac{3}{4}$

    b. $\dfrac{2}{4}$

    c. $\dfrac{2}{8}$

    d. $\dfrac{1}{3}$

    e. Answer cannot be determined

In this case, the GCD is 2. In other words, both 6 and 8 can be divided by 2 without a remainder. 6 divided by 2 is 3. 8 divided by 2 is 4. Furthermore, there is no greater number that would divide into both 6 and 8 without having a remainder. Therefore, the answer is the first choice, 3/4.

Comparing Fractions

One of the most frequent GRE questions involving fractions requires a comparison.

Example: Determine which column is greater in value between the two following fractions:

$$\frac{3}{4} \quad ? \quad \frac{5}{8}$$

Did panic just overcome you? It should not. Just use what is called "the bowtie method."

First, multiply the first denominator (4) by the second numerator (5) and write that answer (4 x 5= 20) above the second fraction. Then, multiply the second denominator by the first numerator, and write that answer above the first fraction (8 x 3= 24). Since 24 (written above 3/4) is greater than 20 (written above 5/8), the answer is

$$\frac{3}{4} > \frac{5}{8}$$

What you're doing is comparing the columns by making each fraction not change its value, while having the same denominator as each other. So, the first fraction becomes 24/32 and the second fraction becomes 20/32.

DECIMALS

Do not worry about seemingly dismal decimals. Decimals are just another version of fractions. Decimals and fractions express the same values in different forms. Why do we use two different forms to express the same values? Variety is the spice of life!

Here are some examples of fractions expressed in decimal form:

.5

.10

.1

To convert a fraction into its decimal equivalent, you must simply divide the numerator by the denominator. Therefore, .75 is the decimal equivalent of 3/4. Do not concern yourself with how this works out visually, in terms of the mathematics. I can assure you that you will not get a GRE test question that asks you the decimal equivalent of 3/4. Moreover, the GRE will not throw a question at you that requires six minutes of longhand division.

You should know how to:

- Add and subtract decimals

- Divide decimals

- Compare decimals

- Identify "digits" that fall after the decimal point

If you do not know how to perform any of the first two functions, you should consult a math textbook or any of the resources listed at the end of this book. As a previous GRE test taker, the most frequent type of questions I saw were the last two.

When comparing decimals, line up the numbers by their decimal points (on your scratch paper) and then fill in the missing zeros.

Example: Determine which is greater in value between 0.00088 and 0.003

Step 1: 0.00088

0.003

Step 2: 0.00088

0.00300

Now you can see which number is larger because 100 is clearly larger than 88.

The GRE also asks you a question about "Digits."

Example: Identify the tenths digit in the number 0.695

To answer these questions, simply memorize the following (consider putting this information on a flashcard to carry around with you and study when possible):

In the above number:

0 is the UNITS digit

6 is the TENTHS digit

9 is the HUNDREDTHS digit

5 is the THOUSANDTHS digit

PERCENTAGES

Percentages are another means by which to express division. They can therefore be converted into fractions or decimals and vice versa. A percentage is a way to symbolize a fraction whose denominator is equal to 100. Percent means "per 100," "out of 100,"or "divided by 100." If your roommate finds a dollar and gives you $.30, he or she has given you 30 cents out of 100, or 3/100 of a dollar. This can also be expressed as 30 percent of a dollar.

Most GRE prep books recommend that you memorize a series of percentage-decimal-fraction equivalents. Since this advice is so popular, I have included my own list below. It is not as extensive as the list given in other prep books because as a previous GRE test taker, I never found memorizing the entire list useful by any means whatsoever. Please also note that most books suggest you memorize these "lists" in an effort to eliminate choices "out of the ballpark" associated with a given question.

- **Tip:** If you know how to answer a particular problem, you do not need to worry about eliminating certain choices. Rather, you will simply solve the problem and identify the sole correct answer.

$$0.1 = \frac{1}{10} = 10\%$$

$0.2 = \dfrac{1}{5} = 20\%$

$0.25 = \dfrac{1}{4} = 25\%$

$0.5 = \dfrac{1}{2} = 50\%$

$0.\overline{6} = \dfrac{2}{3} = 60\%$

$0.75 = \dfrac{3}{4} = 75\%$

$1.0 = \dfrac{1}{1} = 100\%$

For the GRE, you should be able to perform certain functions involving percentages. Be prepared to know how to:

- ✔ Convert decimals to percentages

- ✔ Calculate a percentage increase/decrease

If you need to convert a decimal to a percentage, simply move the decimal point two places to the right.

Example: Problem: Express 0.6 in percent form.

Solution: 0.6…060. = 60%

If you need to find the percentage by which something has decreased or increased, use the following formula:

Percent Change = $\dfrac{\text{Difference}}{\text{Original x 100}}$

The "difference" is then the solution when you subtract the smaller number from the larger. The "original" is the number with which you started.

Example: Problem: Find the percent increase from 4 to 6.

Solution:

1. "Difference" (6 - 4) = 2

2. Original number = 4

3. Percent Change = $\dfrac{2}{4}$ X 100, which is $\dfrac{1}{2}$ (.50) X 100, which

SQUARE ROOTS

Finding the square root of a number is the opposite of squaring the number.

The square root of a number, *n*, as shown below is the number that gives *n* when multiplied by itself.

$$\sqrt{n}$$ equals 50%.

Hence, $\sqrt{4}$, means that a certain value, squared, equals 4.

For the GRE, you should know how to:

✓ Multiply and divide square roots

✓ Estimate and simplify square roots

You multiply and divide square roots just like you would any other numbers.

Therefore, $\sqrt{4} \cdot \sqrt{9} = \sqrt{36} = 6$

When adding and subtracting square roots, you cannot add and subtract them unless the roots are the same. If you need to add and subtract roots, you must first estimate their value and then add or subtract them. To estimate roots, you must be familiar with perfect squares. For example, you know that $\sqrt{25} = 5$ and $\sqrt{36} = 6$, but how do you know what $\sqrt{33}$ is? You must estimate. Clearly, the answer falls somewhere in between $\sqrt{25}$ and $\sqrt{36}$, which means that the answer falls in between 5 and 6. You also know that 33 is closer to 36 than it is to 25, so the answer is closer to 6 than 5. This will allow you to "ballpark" the answer and eliminate choices that are clearly wrong.

Example: Problem: Simplify $\sqrt{33}$

    a. 2
    b. 4.55
    c. 5.01
    d. 5.74
    e. 6.1

You may see a question like this on the GRE, and now you will know the answer. If the answer, based on what you know about perfect squares (see above) is between 5 and 6 and closer to 6 than 5, than the correct answer is the fourth choice, 5.74. If you have time, you can check by squaring the value to see what you get. For example, $5.74 \cdot 5.74 =$ _____

EXPONENTS

Exponents are a type of mathematical shorthand. Instead of writing (3)(3)(3)(3)(3)(3), you can use an exponent and write 3^6. The small 6 is called the "exponent," and 3 is the "base."

ETS® assumes that for the GRE, you know how to:

- ✔ Multiply and divide with exponents

- ✔ Apply other rules of exponents

Essentially, every question that involves exponents on the GRE requires that you know how to apply the rules of exponents:

Here are the rules:

- To multiply two or more numbers with exponents that have the same base, just add the exponents together.

- To divide two or more numbers with exponents that share the same base, subtract the two exponents.

- When there are exponents inside and outside a set of parentheses, just multiply them.

- A negative number raised to an even power always becomes positive. $(-2)^4 = 16$

- A negative number raised to an odd power always remains negative.

- Any number raised to a negative power is equal to 1 over the number raised to the positive power. $2^{-2} = \dfrac{1}{2^2} = \dfrac{1}{4}$

- Any number raised to the power of 0 is always 1.

- Any number raised to the power of 1 is always the number itself.

Do not waste your time studying these concepts extensively. I spent many hours studying pages and pages of intricate details about square roots and exponents from other GRE prep books on the market. These hours and efforts did not assist me in any way on the actual test day. What did assist me was learning the rules and formulas and repeatedly practicing how to apply them, ad nauseum. At the risk of sounding like a broken record, unless you are naturally skilled and adept in math, none of this will do you any good if you are unable to quickly and efficiently churn out answers to problems on test day.

Tip #61: Brush up on your algebra skills.

Here are algebra concepts that you will want to familiarize yourself with for this section of the GRE:

FACTORING

If you rewrite the expression $ab + ac$ in the form $a(b + c)$, you are said to be *factoring* the original expression. Factoring simply means that you isolate the factor common to both terms of the original expression. This new version is the factored version.

Whenever possible on the GRE, use your factoring skills. For example, if you come across a problem you must solve that contains the expression $8x + 8y$, it might be helpful to factor it. This yields the expression $8(x + y)$. This will likely save you time and effort when trying to answer these types of questions.

PROBABILITY

Probability questions can particularly provoke fear in individuals who suffer from math anxiety. Why? Because probability questions on the GRE appear in the form of word problems and anyone who has challenges with math can be afraid of word problems.

If you use the following formula, though, you can answer any question that involves probability. Again, the key to cracking these questions is practice. You can memorize the formula. You can even practice using it once or twice. If you do not do more than that, you will experience a tremendous challenge trying to answer these questions on your GRE. If, though, you know the formula and have practiced answering 30-40 questions like this before your GRE, you will zip right through these questions on the test.

Probability =   number of possible outcomes that satisfy the condition (divided by)

number of total possible outcomes

How to Solve Linear Equations

A linear equation is a mathematical expression that has an equal sign and linear expressions. Examples of linear expressions are $x + 4$ and $2x + 4$. An example of a linear equation is $2x - 1 = 5$. Linear expressions never have exponents or involve square roots or the division of two, separate variables.

If you have an equation that contains only one variable, you can solve for that variable by isolating the variable on one side of the question and the numbers on the other side. Whatever you do to one side of the equation, you must do to the other side.

Example: Solve $2x - 1 = 5$

Solution: $2x - 1 = 5$

       Add 1 to each side

$2x = 6$

Divide each side by 2

$x = 3$

INEQUALITIES

In an equation, one side is equal to the other. In the case of an inequality, one side is not equal to the other. Equations contain equal signs. Inequalities may contain the following:

$\neq$ (is not equal to)

$>$ (is greater than)

$<$ (is less than)

$\geq$ (is greater than or equal to)

$\leq$ (is less than or equal to)

Solve inequalities the same way you solve equations. Isolate the variable on one side of the equation and the numbers on the other side. The only difference is that when you multiply or divide both sides of an inequality by a negative number, you must reverse the direction of the inequality symbol.

HOW TO SOLVE QUADRATIC EQUATIONS

A quadratic equation is a polynomial equation of the second degree. Polynomials are assigned names according to their degree. Polynomials of the first degree are considered "Degree 1," which are "Linear." We already learned about those. The second degree is "Quadratic." You do not need to worry about the degrees beyond the second (such as the third, fourth and fifth) for the GRE. Keep in mind that it is very unusual for a problem to require the Quadratic formula, so it is that much more important to familiarize yourself with the previous two strategies.

A quadratic equation in symbolic form looks like this:

$ax^2 + bx + c = 0$

You can solve these problems by:

- Factoring

- Solving for a variable

- Using the quadratic formula:

$$\frac{-b \pm \sqrt{(b^2 - 4ac)}}{2a}$$

**Tip #62: Memorize algebraic formulas
that you will need to know for the test.**

I highly recommend that you memorize formulas which relate to algebra before the test. You cannot write down any formulas before the test in the ETS® testing center itself. You can, however, use your test time whichever way you want. Therefore, if you want to take a few moments during the test to jot down some important formulas, this may prove useful.

Algebraic Formulas Cheat Sheet:

I. Binomial Theorem

- $(a + b)^1 = a + b$

- $(a + b)^2 = a^2 + 2ab + b^2$

- $(a + b)^3 = a^3 + 3a^2b + 3ab^2 + b^3$

- $(a + b)^4 = a^4 + 4a^3b + 6a^2b^2 + 4ab^3 + b^4$ ...and so on...

II. Difference of Squares

- $a^2 - b^2 = (a - b)(a + b)$

III. Quadratic Formula

In an equation like $ax^2 + bx + c = 0$

You can solve for x using the Quadratic Formula:

$$\frac{-b \pm \sqrt{b^2 - 4ac}}{2a}$$

III. "Laws" or "Rules" of Exponents:

- $(a^m)(a^n) = a^{m+n}$

- $(ab)^m = a^m b^m$

- $(a^m)^n = a^{mn}$

- $a^{m/n} = \sqrt[n]{a^m}$

- $a^0 = 1$

- $(a^m)/(a^n) = a^{m-n}$

- $a^{-m} = 1/(a^m)$

"The Rules of Zero"

- $0/x = 0$ where x is not equal to 0.

- $a/0$ is undefined (you cannot————do it)

- $a^0 = 1$

- $0^a = 0$

- $a \bullet 0 = 0$

Again, just try and memorize these formulas. You should also practice with them.

Tip #63: Practice GRE Test algebra-type problems.

At the end of this chapter, you can find practice problems that will require you to use your algebra skills. You can also go to the ETS® Web site and download more. Do I sound like a broken record? Sorry, but again, it does not matter how well you know your algebra. You must practice over and over again so that you can run on auto-pilot when your GRE test day arrives.

Tip #64: What to do if you are not sure how to solve a problem.

Most GRE prep books on the market do give tips and strategies to help you solve algebraic conundrums if you are unsure of how to do the math. I will share a few of those tips with you but not without a disclaimer.

- **Tip:** My disclaimer is that using alternative means (like working backwards or resorting to a strategy that involves "plugging in" numbers) may work but will cost you valuable time. It is preferable for you to study hard for the test, practice problems over and over again, and then know how to find solutions to the problems presented to you on test day. While some of these tips and strategies may work, you should be aware of the following:

- If you do not know how to answer a problem, you will immediately get stressed out.

- You will then attempt to use one of your "strategies" for solving a problem when you do not know how to solve it.

- You may or may not be successful afterwards, depending on how nervous you are while you attempt your tips and strategies.

MATH STRATEGIES

I. Working Backwards

If you do need to set up and solve an equation to find an answer to a GRE question and do not know how to do so, you can try working backward. You can use this strategy when you are asked to solve an equation in symbolic or word problem form. Do this by running the answers through the equation in the question until you find the one that works.

Here is the "how to" for working backwards:

- Start with the third answer choice (C). The reason for this is that the choice with the most middle value is usually (C). The values tend to be in order of quantity, either least to greatest, or greatest to least.

- Eliminate answers that are too big or too small. If (C) is too small, everything less than (C) must also be too small. If (C) is too big, then everything greater than (C) is also too big.

- Go through the remaining answers for a question until you find the right one.

II. Plugging In Numbers

Use this strategy if you do not know how to answer a question and you are working with percents, fractions, or ratios.

Here is the "how to" for plugging in:

- Pick a simple number to replace the variables. Choose a number like 8 or 20, not 107, unless you are trying to answer a question involving percents, in which case always use 100.

- Plug the number you selected into the equations. The result is your target number.

- Plug your chosen number into the answer choices, eliminating those that do not yield your target number.

Tip #65: Brush up on your geometry skills.

You will have some questions that relate to geometry on the GRE. Remember, ETS® will only test your high school level of knowledge and proficiency. You just need to brush up on your knowledge and skills, memorize formulas, and then practice answering problems. Please be sure that you do not let other GRE prep books confuse you and obstruct you from answering geometrical problems on the GRE. I am not one to name names. It should suffice to say, though, that one of the books on the GRE prep book market has a sentence in it which states you do not need to know much about geometry to do well on the GRE. I ask you: How can this be? If the GRE presents you with questions which involve the application of geometrical formulas and application skills, how can it be that you do not actually need to know much about geometry to score well on the GRE? The answer is that the statement from the other book is misleading at minimum and also potentially false. I have often pondered why GRE prep books would promulgate such misleading statements to students who seek to score higher on the GRE. I have not come to any conclusions. Please do not be lured into thinking that there are shortcuts or ways to circumvent learning what you need to do for any part of the GRE, including any questions that involve geometry. Although it is true that you do not need an extensive array of knowledge regarding all things geometrical; the statement that you do not need to know much about geometry itself is blatantly false.

ANGLES, LINES, AND DEGREES

ETS will expect you to know the following for the GRE:

- The sum of a large angle and a small angle is always 180 degrees.

- When two lines intersect, four angles are formed. The sum of these four angles = 360 degrees.

- When two lines are perpendicular to each other, their intersection forms four 90-degree angles. The ETS® is generous in this regard; it will tell you when angles are perpendicular. This is the symbol that ETS® uses to indicate a perpendicular angle. $\perp$

- Ninety-degree angles are also referred to as right-angles. Again, ETS® will clearly indicate any right angles to you on the exam. Look for this symbol: ∟

- The three angles inside any triangle add up to 180 degrees.

- The four angles inside a four-sided figure (such as a square or rectangle) always add up to 360 degrees.

- Vertical angles are always equal.

- When two parallel lines (//) intersect with a third line, two types of angles are formed: large and small. The large angles formed are always equal, as are the small. Moreover, the sum of any large and small angles is always 180 degrees.

Triangles

ETS will expect you to know the following about triangles for the exam:

- All triangles contain three angles that add up to 180 degrees, regardless of the type of triangle.

- There are three types of common triangles tested on the GRE.

1. **Equilateral Triangles:** A triangle in which all three sides equal in length and consequently, all angles are equal. Since all triangles have three angles that add up to 180 degrees and equilateral triangles contain

angles of equal degrees; equilateral triangles all have three, 60 degree angles.

2. **Isosceles Triangles:** A triangle in which two of the three sides are equal in length (hence two of the angles are also equal).

3. **Right Triangles:** A triangle in which one angle is a right angle (90 degrees.)

-   In any given triangle, the longest side is opposite the largest interior angle. Conversely, the shortest side is opposite the smallest interior angle. Moreover, the third side of a triangle can never be longer than the sum of the other two sides. Nor can it be shorter than the difference of the other two sides.

-   You can determine the perimeter of a triangle by adding up all of its sides, since the perimeter is simply a measure of the distance around it.

-   You will also want to know how to determine the area of a triangle. See the formulas section that follows.

Circles

You will only see a few questions regarding circles on the GRE. ETS® will expect you to know the following about circles:

-   That $\pi = 3.14159$, but you may round this to 3 for the purposes of answering GRE questions.

-   That the radius of a circle is any line that extends from the center to the edge of the circle and the diameter goes through the entire circle's center.

-   How to determine the area of a circle (see the formula list).

- How to determine the circumference of a circle (see the formula list that follows).

Again, although memorizing all of the formulas will help you on test day, unless you have repeatedly practiced how to quickly and efficiently apply the formulas, you may find yourself spending an extraneous amount of time trying to answer a geometry question that involves circles.

THE COORDINATE SYSTEM

You may see a few questions regarding the coordinate system on the GRE. ETS® will expect you to know the following:

- On a coordinate system, the horizontal line is called the x-axis. The vertical axis is called the y-axis. The four areas formed by the intersection of these axes are called quadrants. The point at which all axes intersect is called the origin.

Example:

Points on a coordinate system are expressed in parentheses, with the horizontal value expressed first and the vertical second (x, y).

SLOPE

More than likely, you will receive at least one or two GRE coordinate system test questions that involve calculating the slope of a line.

The equation for a line is expressed symbolically as $y = mx + b$; whereas both x and y are points on a line, b stands for the y-intercept and m is the slope of the line.

"Slope" is defined as the vertical change divided by the horizontal change. This is sometimes expressed as "the rise over the run," or "the change in y over the change in x." You can calculate the slope on any GRE question with the following formula:

$$m= \frac{y2 - y1}{x2 - x1}$$

In other words, given two points $(x1, y1)$ and $(x2, y2)$, the change in x from one to the other is $x2 - x1$, while the change in y is $y2 - y1$. The above formula simply expresses this in symbolic form.

Again, memorizing this formula is not the only thing that will help you answer a test question. You may remember the formula but then panic as you try and figure out what to do with it. You need to practice with real questions. Also, if this concept or any others are completely foreign to you, you must consult a mathematics text book and conduct further research. Alternatively, you can hire a tutor. This is simply a review of the basic concepts that ETS assumes you know. The application of these concepts is the key to your success on test day.

Tip #66: Memorize any geometry formulas you will need on test day.

GEOMETRY FORMULAS CHEAT SHEET

Formulas for flat, two-dimensional shapes

I. Area of a rectangle

(Length • Width)

A = *lw*

II. Perimeter of a rectangle

(The sum of the top and bottom lengths and left and right widths)

P = 2*l* + 2*w*

III. Area of a square

(Side measurement squared)

A = s²

IV. Perimeter of a square

(Length of side • 4)

P = 4s

V. Area of a triangle

$$A = \left(\frac{1}{2}\right) bh$$

VI. Perimeter of a triangle

(Sum of lengths of the three sides)

Side 1 + Side 2 + Side 3 = P

VII. Area of a circle, given the radius *r*

A = π *r*²

π is the number approximated by 3.14159.

Radius (r) is the distance from the center of the circle to its outside. If you are given a diameter in a problem (the length of a line going all the way across a circle, as opposed to half-way across), you will divide the number in half and then apply these formulas).

VIII. Circumference of a circle

$C = 2\pi r$

Formulas for three-dimensional shapes

I. Volume of a cube

$V = s^3$

II. Formula for the surface area of a cube (the area you would measure if you needed to paint outside a cube)

$SA = 6s^2$

III. Volume of a rectangular prism

(Length • Width • Height)

$V = lwh$

VI. Surface area for a rectangular prism

$SA = 2lw + 2wh + 2lh$

VII. Volume of a cylinder

(Area of the end—or area of the circle) times the height

$V = \pi r^2 h$

VIII. Surface area of a cylinder

(Area of ends, plus the area of the side)

$SA = 2\pi r^2 + 2\pi rh$

IX. Volume of a cone, with radius r and height h

$$V^{cone} = \frac{1}{3}\pi r^2 h$$

Although it is not a formula, you should be familiar with the Pythagorean Theorem, which applies only to right triangles. A right triangle is a triangle in which one of the angles is a right angle (= to 90 degrees). The longest side of a right triangle (opposite the 90 degree angle) is called the hypotenuse. The Pythagorean Theorem states that in a right triangle, the square of the hypotenuse's length equals the sum of the squares of the length of the two other sides.

$c^2 = a^2 + b^2$, where c equals the length of the hypotenuse.

Tip #67: Practice GRE Test geometry problems.

You can find questions to practice with at the end of the chapter. Then, you can go to the ETS® Web site and download more questions. Remember, as I have said with other mathematical concepts, memorizing all of the formulas will not serve you well on test day unless you know how to quickly and efficiently apply them. The only means by which you can learn to aptly and speedily apply the right formula and solve a problem is to practice.

Tip #68: Guess "C" if you are not sure how to solve a geometry problem.

Unfortunately, there are no ways to cut corners on geometry problems. If you are unsure how to solve a problem involving geometry, you are best advised to guess the third answer choice. You could also attempt to quickly scan the problem and eliminate any answer choices that look totally out of the question, based on what you know. Solving geometry problems, however, involves applying geometry formulas. There is no substitute for knowledge and experience in this realm.

Tip #69: Brush up on and Practice GRE data interpretation questions.

Some of the 28 questions in the quantitative section are questions that involve data interpretation. Be careful. If you are using other GRE prep books to study for the GRE, some of them contain incorrect information about this portion of the test. Some of these books state that you will only receive four data interpretation questions and that you will receive the questions in two sets of two questions each. This is not correct. You will receive more than four data interpretation questions, though the exact number is unknown. Also, the questions will appear in sets of two to five questions. Although the data is occasionally represented in a chart or table, you will most frequently (if not always) see the data represented graphically on the GRE. The most common types of graphs used on the GRE are:

- Line graphs

- Bar graphs

- Circle graphs

Also, remember how I warned you about this section of the test? Again, I know what you are thinking: "I can read a graph; I do not need to study about how to read graphs." I do not want to sound repetitive, but the key to acing this section is practice. While other books on the market may tell you that these questions involve the application of mathematical concepts, as opposed to visually assessing numerical data presented on the screen in front of you, the cases in which you will actually need to perform complex mathematical operations for this section are few and far between. At the risk of sounding simplistic, this section is called data interpretation for a reason. As a previous GRE test taker, I can assure you that excessively studying mathematical operations will not assist you with this section of the test. I have another note to share with you regarding data interpretation calculations.

- **Tip:** Although calculations are required for this section of the GRE, remember that you cannot use a calculator for the test. Therefore, ETS® will not present you with any question that requires extensive calculations. If you ever see a situation in which you can estimate, take advantage of this opportunity and do so. If you ever find yourself attempting to answer a data interpretation question and find yourself engaged in lengthy and complicated calculations, stop. Realize that you are on the wrong track. Take a step back, look at the graph and tackle the question again.

When answering data interpretation questions, always:

- Quickly scan the data to see what it concerns without attempting to analyze every aspect of the graph or chart.

- Check for any relevant notes related to the data.

- Look at the questions.

- Go back to the data (on the chart or graph) and focus on the aspects which will assist you in answering the questions.

- If possible, estimate. Never perform lengthy calculations.

- Only base your answers on the data present and your application of mathematical skills.

Some examples of mathematical operations you may need to perform on this section are how to:

- ✔ Calculate percentages.

te percentage increases or decreases.

study excessively for this section of the test. Do practice. At the end of this chapter, you can find a practice question to try. You can follow up this question with more from the ETS® Web site. Also, if you download the ETS® study guide, you will notice how little space the data interpretation section of the study guide takes up.

Practice Problems for Arithmetic (easy)

1. Add 0.99 + 45.102 + 0.00002

    A. 48.241
    B. 452.009
    C. 46.09202
    D. 248.092
    E. 146.920

2. Find 0.13 ÷ 1

    A. 13
    B. 1.3
    C. .13
    D. .013
    E. .0013

3. (12 ÷ 4) x (6 ÷ 2) =

    A. 1
    B. 9
    C. 72
    D. 576
    E. 752

4. 5 x 0 x 4

    A. 20
    B. 9
    C. 15
    D. 0
    E. 10

5. 7.95 ÷ 1.5

    A. 2.4
    B. 5.3
    C. 6.2
    D. 7.3
    E. 7.5

6. -33 + 8 equals:

    A. -25
    B. 25
    C. -26
    D. 26
    E. 27

7. -38 + -48 equals:

    A. 10
    B. -86
    C. 84
    D. 77
    E. 68

8. 31 percent equals:

    A. 3.1
    B. .31
    C. .031
    D. .0031
    E. .00315

ANSWER KEY	
1. C	5. B
2. C	6. A
3. B	7. B
4. D	8. B

PRACTICE PROBLEMS FOR ALGEBRA (EASY–HARD)

SET ONE

1. If Missy can paint a house in 4 hours, and Mike can paint the same house in 6 hours, how long will it take for both of them to paint the house together?

    A. 2 hours and 24 minutes
    B. 3 hours and 12 minutes
    C. 3 hours and 44 minutes
    D. 4 hours and 10 minutes
    E. 4 hours and 33 minutes

2. Employees of a retail merchandising store receive an additional 15 percent off of the lowest price on an item. If an employee purchases a bedspread during a 20 percent off sale, how much will he or she pay if the dishwasher originally cost $450?

    A. $280.90
    B. $287
    C. $292.50
    D. $306
    E. $333.89

3. The sales price of a car is $16,533.18, which is 15 percent off the original price. What was the original price?

   A. $16,533.18   D. $19,450.80
   B. $18,695.40   E. $17,360.20
   C. $19,890.50

4. If Casey is six years older than her friend, Lisa, and John is five years older than Casey, and the total of their ages is 41, then what is Lisa's age?

   A. 8   D. 19
   B. 10   E. 21
   C. 14

5. Alfred wants to invest $3,000 at a 5 percent simple interest rate for five years. How much interest will he receive?

   A. $75   D. $600
   B. $120   E. $750
   C. $240

6. Bob is able to sell a wood desk for $494.25 which was a 25 percent profit over his cost. How much did the desk cost him to build?

   A. $380.65   D. $475.20
   B. $395.40   E. $510.30
   C. $420.60

ANSWER KEY	
1. A	4. A
2. D	5. E
3. D	6. B

SET TWO

1. Assume that the average of three numbers is A. If one of the numbers is B and another is C, what is the remaining number?

    A. BC - A   D. 3A – B – C
    B. B/A – 3 - C   E. A – B – C
    C. B/3 – A – C

2. John can fill a pool carrying pails of water in 30 minutes. Mary can perform the same task in 45 minutes. Lisa can do the same job in 1 ½ hours. How fast can John, Mary and Lisa all fill the pool together?

    A. 12 minutes   D. 23 minutes
    B. 15 minutes   E. 28 minutes
    C. 21 minutes

3. Which of the following is not a rational number?

    A. -2   D. 0.25
    B. $\dfrac{2}{5}$ E. Square of 2

    C. $.2\overline{5}$

4. Mark is traveling to a seminar that is 28 miles away. He needs to be there in 30 minutes or he will be late. How fast does Mark need to travel make it to the seminar on time?

    A. 25 mph   D. 49 mph
    B. 37 mph   E. 56 mph
    C. 41 mph

5. Multiply 106 by 104

    A. 10,104   D. 10,102

B. 10,010   E. 10,120

C. 10,124

6. Divide x^6 by x^3

    A. x^3 D. x^3

    B. x^{18} E. x^1

    C. x^6

ANSWER KEY:	
1. D	4. E
2. B	5. C
3. E	6. A

PRACTICE PROBLEMS FOR GEOMETRY

1. If a circle has the diameter of 8, which of the following numbers represents the circumference?

    A. 6.39   D. 40.14

    B. 13.56   E. 100.38

    C. 25.13

2. Which of the following letters corresponds to the vertex in the following picture?

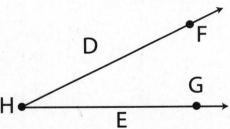

    A. D and E   D. G only

B. E and H   E. H only

C. F and G

3. What is the area of a triangle with a base of 12 cm and a height of cm?

A. 33 cm^2 D. 60 cm^2

B. 42 cm^2 E. 74 cm^2

C. 54cm^2

4. What is the measure of angle B in the following figure if angle A measures 120°?

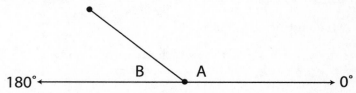

A. 55°   D. 120°

B. 60°   E. 270°

C. 65°

ANSWER KEY:	
1. C	3. B
2. E	4. B

Although there are not as many questions that relate to Geometry on the GRE as there are algebra questions, you should continue to practice your skills by procuring more questions at **www.ets.org.**

PRACTICE PROBLEMS QUANTITATIVE COMPARISON QUESTIONS

1. a + b = 15

a – b = 24

COLUMN A	COLUMN B
-(a)	a-(-5)

A. if the quantity in Column A is greater

B. if the quantity in Column B is greater

C. if the two quantities are equal

D. if it is impossible to determine which quantity is greater

2.

COLUMN A	COLUMN B
The area of a circle with the radius of 4	The area of a semi-circle with the radius of 5

A. if the quantity in Column A is greater

B. if the quantity in Column B is greater

C. if the two quantities are equal

D. if it is impossible to determine which quantity is greater

3.

COLUMN A	COLUMN B
The fraction of 152 hours of a week	The fraction of 20 hours in a day

A. if the quantity in Column A is greater

B. if the quantity in Column B is greater

C. if the two quantities are equal

D. if it is impossible to determine which quantity is greater

4.

COLUMN A	COLUMN B
500 percent of five	600 percent of four

A. if the quantity in Column A is greater

B. if the quantity in Column B is greater

C. if the two quantities are equal

D. if it is impossible to determine which quantity is greater

ANSWER KEY:	
1. A	3. A
2. A	4. A

PRACTICE PROBLEM FOR DATA ANALYSIS/ INTERPRETATION QUESTIONS

1. If Awesome Auto Outlet sold 39,000 vehicles in 2009, how many SUVs did they sell?

Awesome Auto Outlet Sales 2009

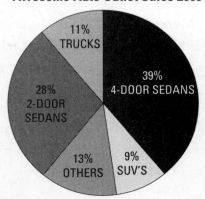

    A. 2,985   D. 3,650

    B. 3,510   E. 3,680

    C. 3,590

2. If 3,850 trucks were sold in 2009, how many total vehicles were sold in 2008 by Awesome Auto Outlet?

    A. 28,000   D. 40,000

    B. 30,000   E. 50,000

    C. 35,000

3. If 3,360 2-door sedans were sold in 2009, then how many 4-door sedans were sold in 2008 by Awesome Auto Sales?

    A. 4,680   D. 5,470

    B. 5,010   E. 5,490

    C. 5,250

ANSWER KEY:		
1. B	2. C	3. A

New Question Type: Numeric Entry

This is the other type of new question that ETS® began to introduce in November of 2007. Again, at the time of this publication, ETS® has not released these test questions as "official" questions that count toward a given test taker's score. Moreover, ETS® owns the copyright to all of the strategies for these types of questions it has not yet released. You may or may not encounter this question type, depending on when you take the GRE.

At the time of this publication, ETS® offers a brief online guide with a few strategies and practice questions. I encourage you to visit **www.ets.org** immediately to review this type of test question.

You should know the following about these questions:

- These questions will require that your answer is a number in a single box or is a fraction in two separate boxes (one for the numerator and one for the denominator).

- For a single answer box, you will type in the answer box using the keyboard.

- Once you click on the answer box, a cursor will appear within the box. You just type in your numerical answer. (Note: this is not multiple choice).

- Use a hyphen to indicate a negative sign, if needed.

- Round your answer only if specifically asked to do so. Otherwise, enter your exact answer.

- Fractions do not need to be expressed in simplified form.

At the time of this publication, ETS® offers a brief online guide with a few strategies and practice questions. Visit **www.ets.org** immediately to review this type of test question.

CHAPTER 10 HOMEWORK

1. Formulate your plan for how you will practice your math skills. Start by going to **www.ets.org** and downloading a full length practice test. This will allow you to evaluate your strengths and weaknesses.

2. Study for each aspect of the math section according to your study schedule, but build in extra time to compensate for honing the skills required to strengthen your weak areas.

3. In addition to the practice questions in this book, use the software

(which includes tutorials, practice questions and full-length practice tests) for more practice.

CHAPTER 11

How to Prepare for the Analytical Writing Section of the GRE

The analytical writing section of the GRE can seem like the easiest or most challenging section for which to prepare. Some people find it challenging to get ready for it because they simply do not like to write. Unfortunately, the idea that the analytical writing section of the GRE only tests writing is a myth, not the truth. Scientists and engineers who do not like to write can certainly score well on this portion of the test. Conversely, English majors who plan to rest on their laurels or who think that they are "good writers" and therefore do not need to prepare, may find themselves receiving a much lower score than they expected.

I have scored a 6.0 — the highest possible score — on the analytical writing section of the GRE and am here to encourage you to aim for that score as well. I know what you might be thinking: "Well, she is a writer, so of course she scored a 6.0." Although my interest in writing may have assisted me somewhat on this portion of the test, it did not earn me a perfect score. Despite my affinity for writing, I studied for and practiced answering questions for the analytical writing section for many long, grueling hours. I did not intend to rest on my laurels, so I formulated a study plan and stuck to it. You can do the same.

Next, I am going to teach you the secrets behind what this section is all about. The most important thing for you to understand is that the essay scorers of the analytical writing section do not expect for you to just plop down and type out your opinions and ruminations for an hour and fifteen minutes. This is a good thing, actually, because the essay scorers are looking for specific aspects of a good essay. You can provide them with that if you study and practice.

**Tip #70: Get your basics in order:
punctuation, grammar, and time management.**

PUNCTUATION AND GRAMMAR

You should take time to review grammar and punctuation before you take the GRE. Spark Notes publishes an easily accessible and user friendly grammar chart, which you can purchase online for only $4.95. See **www. sparknotes.com** or check your local bookstore.

Yes, it is true: Grammar and punctuation do not play a large role in your score on the analytical writing section of the GRE, since a holistic criterion is applied to assess and assign your score. The term *holistic*, in this sense, means that the two graders who read your essay will look at *all* aspects of your essay, including grammar, style, mechanics, content, logical progression, and more. Your grammar and punctuation will not "make" or "break" you on this section of the exam, but it could help or hurt you. You can write a conceptually brilliant essay, but if it is riddled with grammar and punctuation problems, your score will be marked down appropriately. Conversely, an essay of average conceptual content with impeccable grammar and mechanics may be viewed more favorably than a weak essay with a plethora of grammar errors.

The ETS® professionals who read your essays are supposed to ignore minor grammar, spelling, and punctuation errors. They do realize that you are writing these essays under pressure and under timed circumstances. This does not give you a license to be careless, though.

- **A quick tip:** The College of Arts and Sciences at Illinois State University hosts an excellent Web site, which serves as an excellent source for punctuation help: **http://lilt.ilstu.edu/golson/punctuation/**

This Web site, titled "Punctuation Made Simple" by Gary Olson, is worth your time to at least walk through. Olson *does* make punctuation simple and you can go through all the lessons in about an hour and 15 minutes.

ORGANIZATION

When practicing and writing your actual essays, keep organization in mind. Do not just sit down and "shoot from the hip" and write whatever comes to mind. Make an outline of what you plan to write. This is essential, particularly once you understand the components that must be in these essays. By taking the time to sketch an outline on paper, you will not forget to put something critical in your essay that you might have otherwise forgotten under the pressure of the nerve-racking GRE testing environment.

TIME MANAGEMENT

You *must* have a plan. If you just sit down to outline, write, and then see what happens, you will run out of time and/or not have time to proofread your essay before the clock runs out. Prior to when you start writing, decide how much time you need, then watch the clock to make sure that you stick to it.

When you take the "Present Your Perspective on an Issue" section, you will receive 45 minutes in which to write your essay. Take five to six minutes for brief planning and outlining, set aside 35 minutes for writing, and then reserve four to five minutes for brief proofreading at the end of your writing session time.

When you take the "Analyze an Argument" section, you will receive 30 minutes in which to write your essay. I advise that you take four to five minutes for planning and outlining, set aside 20 minutes for writing, and then reserve four to five minutes for proofreading at the end of your writing session time.

All of these aspects of time management are equally important. If you do not take the time to develop a plan or outline, you will find yourself aimlessly writing. Then, halfway through your essay, you may realize that you have no idea what you are talking about or where you are going with this essay. Conversely, you do not want to spend so much time planning that you then lack the time necessary to fill in your outline. As for proofreading, this step is essential; do not skip it. At this point, you will not be proofreading to perfect your essay. Rather, you will be checking for any glaring errors like typos, not capitalizing the beginning of a sentence or not indenting a paragraph.

If you follow these time management steps, you will find that: (1) You do not feel as anxious about taking this section of the exam, because you know exactly how you are going to tackle it; (2) Your essay will be coherent and logical because you took the time to plan and outline it; (3) You will not need to worry that you have glaring errors in your essay because you simply ran out of time at the end.

Tip #71: Understand the assignment.

The GRE analytical writing section is *not* a podium for you to speak your mind. The people who score your essay do not actually care about your perspective on an issue. Moreover, they are not concerned about their opinion concerning your critique of a particular argument. This is not personal. This is not the time and place to "sound off." It is the time and place to write a good, solid, logical, and coherent essay.

The Issue task states an opinion on a broad interest and asks test-takers to address the issue from any perspective they want. ETS® would like for you to support your opinion on the issue with relevant examples and evidence.

The Argument task requires you to critique an argument by discussing how well reasoned it is. You must consider the logical soundness of the argument, rather than just agree or disagree.

**Tip #72: Think about philosophy because it
will help you with this portion of the test.**

Do you know anything about philosophy? If so, this will help you. If not, listen closely and you can receive the same benefit. Those who have studied philosophy know that philosophers must consider both the pros and cons of any particular issue. Philosophers are particularly adept in the skill of looking at a single issue from multiple points of view. Philosophers also demonstrate aptness in defending either point of view. One of my primary areas of study in graduate school was philosophy. What we do in philosophy, when writing a paper for instance, is:

- Analyze an argument or theory from a philosopher

- Provide a concise and sophisticated summary of that argument

- Critique the argument and give our opinion (or a revised theory)

- Identify possible objections to our opinion or point of view

- Anticipate and address those objections

In my opinion, following this structural format for writing an essay is how

I scored so high on the analytical writing section of the GRE and how *you* can too. Whether I was presenting my perspective or analyzing an argument, I always tried to keep these primary points in mind.

Tip #73: Address the issue task by thinking critically and writing well.

There are a number of ways you can respond to the issue you choose to write about. You can agree or disagree. You can select parts of the issue that you agree with and other parts that you do not. You can qualify a response based on the terms of the issue by writing "If this, then that" statements. You can take a situational approach to the issue by stating under what circumstances it could or could not be supported.

It is important to realize that the readers who score the GRE are not looking for a single correct answer because there is no single correct answer. In this case, what you say is not as important as how you say it. The GRE scoring team will be evaluating how skillfully you write rather than correctness of the position you take.

This is an exercise in critical thinking. To start, you must read the claim or issue statement carefully. Then, you need to think about it from several different perspectives and apply the issue statement to as many different situations as you can imagine.

For example, under what conditions would the sale of cigarettes to a minor be acceptable? If you find no acceptable conditions under which cigarettes should be sold to a minor, you will need to state that, list your reasons for taking that position and support each one. For example, "There is never a time or situation in which selling cigarettes to a minor can be seen as socially and morally acceptable. It is clearly illegal to make such a sale as the signs posted in every store indicate. Moreover, sales clerks are required by the same law to ask for identification if the purchaser appears to be underage." You should also anticipate possible objections to your perspective and address them, like in this example, "Some people find it socially and morally acceptable to sell cigarettes to minors because they feel that if the issue is a moral one, then minors have an equal right to make the same moral "mistakes" as do adults. Minors differ in cognitive capacity and capability, though. Therefore, the issue is not so much about 'rights' as it is about protecting minors from making decisions that they are not fully capable of making yet on an informed basis."

EXAMPLE

Let us pretend that the test asks you to present your perspective on the following issue:

"An author should be judged on the complete body of his or her work, rather than on one outstanding example."

The GRE essay scorers are not looking for a "yes" or "no" here, nor do they expect to receive a simplified version of your opinion. All they are looking for is a good essay. Here is a sample outline of the above question:

A. Your perspective on the issue (a thesis statement)

B. Why you have this perspective

C. One or two examples from history or your own personal experience that support your perspective

D. A "counterexample" or "objection" that would jeopardize your position (someone or something with a conflicting view)

E. An answer to the above objection that shows why your perspective is right, in this case

Now you can see how little of the essay actually involves what you think and how much of it is about the structure and hitting each of the five points listed above. Although your opinion or perspective is important and critical to fully answering the question, it cannot possibly account for the full answer that ETS® wants to read.

Also, remember how critical your four to five minutes of planning and outlining time is. You cannot possibly pull off a sophisticated essay with these five components by just winging it. You must quickly decide your perspective, determine why you have that perspective, consider what examples you will cite to support your position, determine what objections others might have against your view, and then skillfully and efficiently decide how you can overcome those objections, which will subsequently further uphold and support your perspective.

As with the other sections of the GRE, practice does make perfect. It is not easy — even for the experienced writer — to sit down and write an essay, like this, in 45 minutes. The time will pass by quickly. If you practice writing this type of essay at least ten times before test day, by the time you go to actually take the real analytical writing section of the GRE, it will be just another day in your life of writing an essay in 45 minutes. You will have done it so many times already, that it will feel like second nature to you.

You can find more sample questions at the end of this chapter. You can also check the ETS® Web site for sample questions as well.

> **Tip #74: Dissect the argument task.**

The argument task is actually another critical thinking assignment that requires a written response. You are required to read a passage and respond to it in writing. Your written response must address an academic audience. This audience expects to read a response that is organized, well-developed, and uses a variety of syntactical forms and vocabulary with facility. The readers are looking for your insight and understanding of the passage and your skill at expressing those thoughts in writing.

Remember, the GRE is a standardized test given to a large number of prospective graduate students. This is the puzzle piece that tells you the argument passages are selected to elicit your skill at writing, not your content area knowledge. If you are planning to study biology, there is no reason to fear that the argument-writing test is looking for expert content knowledge of philosophy. All of the argument passages are designed for general audiences with an undergraduate education. Again, this is much more about writing a good, structured essay than it is about what you think or what your opinions are.

EXAMPLE

Here is an example of how to tackle a question from the Argument task section of the GRE.

"Recently, the mayor of Seattle released a memo stating that police patrol would be increased downtown at night because crime has increased downtown between the months of October of last year and April of this year. The increase in police patrol will decrease the crime downtown and simultaneously allow this area to flourish again, since residents will subsequently deal with less crime."

This is an example outline/plan/attack for this argument:

A. First state in precise terms exactly what this argument says. Yes, even though it is right above in the question, repeat it. Repeat it, though, in a manner that shows you understand each of the components of the argument. Break things down. This will serve as your introduction. Write something like, "The mayor stated the following things in a recent memo to her staff: (1) That she plans to increase police patrol downtown at night; (2) That the crime has decreased downtown since

October of last year and April of this year; (3) That the increase in police patrol will decrease crime; (4) That the increase in police patrol will also result in a re-flourishing of the downtown area.

B. Then state precisely what is *missing* from the argument (or memo, in this case). Write something like, "The following information was not contained in the memo from the mayor: (1) A date that indicates when the memo was written; (2) When police patrol would be increased in downtown; (3) Any supporting data or statistics that support the claims within the argument.

- **Tip:** There is always something missing from the argument, if not several things. That is the entire point of this section of the analytical writing portion of the GRE. ETS® wants to test your critical thinking skills. Can you find the missing pieces that are necessary to put an entire puzzle together?

C. Next, analyze the argument based only on the above information that you just carved out. Do not say, "I think this argument is good," or "I think this argument is bad." As an example, write something like, "Based on the fact that the mayor outlines a clear action plan but does not provide information that may be pertinent, such as supporting statistics, I would suggest that the mayor's memo possesses potential as a strong argument, but needs supporting data to strengthen and qualify it."

D. Then discuss in more detail why the missing information is critical. As a suggestion, write something like, "Since there is no date on this memo, we do not know when the mayor wrote it. What if she is writing this memo in July and the crime has already decreased since April? Also, the mayor does not provide relevant data or statistics. What if crime customarily increases between October and April every year? What if other reasons exist for the increase in crime? What data supports increased police patrol as a method of effectively reducing crime? Are there other efficient methods that should be considered? What makes this one particular method, which the mayor has chosen, the best? Also, the mayor insinuates that the increase in police patrol will lead to a flourishing of the crime-ridden area. Without supporting statistics, though, this conclusion is not necessarily logical. The mayor does not provide any information that directly links an increased police patrol to decreased crime, nor does she cite any evidence to indicate that a decrease in crime will subsequently result in a particular area experiencing improvements. What if other reasons (besides crime) have contributed to the degeneration of the particular area? In that case, if crime is irrelevant, the mayor's measures will have no effect on whether the area flourishes."

E. Next, tie everything together via a brief conclusion. It is not preferable to begin your conclusion with the words, "In conclusion." As an example, you might write, "Again, the mayor's memo provides information about a crime reduction method that may have significant potential. If relevant data and statistics are procured to support her method and suggestion, the mayor's argument can be strengthened."

Tip #75: Practice writing argument topics and issue topics.

This tip is easy to follow because ETS® publishes a generous amount of sample topics for both portions of the analytical writing section. Follow these steps to get there:

1. Go to **www.ets.org**

2. Under "Tests," click on "GRE."

3. Under "Test Takers," click on "Prepare for the Test(s)."

4. Click the bulletin point for "GRE General Test."

5. Click the tab for "Writing topics."

6. Then, click on what you would like to do — look at the directions or view the pool of topics for this portion of the test.

A few samples are below, and on the following page.

ANALYTICAL WRITING PRACTICE QUESTIONS

ISSUE TOPICS (from the pool at **www.ets.org**)

Present your perspective on the issue below, using relevant reasons and/or examples to support your views.

"Important truths begin as outrageous, or at least uncomfortable, attacks upon the accepted wisdom of the time."

"Originality does not mean thinking something that was never thought before; it means putting old ideas together in new ways."

"Laws should not be rigid or fixed. Instead, they should be flexible enough to take account of various circumstances, times, and places."

"It is always an individual who is the impetus for innovation; the details may be worked out by a team, but true innovation results from the enterprise and unique perception of an individual."

"The function of science is to reassure; the purpose of art is to upset. Therein lies the value of each."

"The study of an academic discipline alters the way we perceive the world. After studying the discipline, we see the same world as before, but with different eyes."

ARGUMENT TOPICS (also from the pool of topics at **www.ets.org**)

Present your perspective on the issue below, using relevant reasons and/or examples to support your views.

Discuss how well reasoned you find this argument.

A recent study shows that people living on the continent of North America suffer 9 times more chronic fatigue and 31 times more chronic depression than do people living on the continent of Asia. Interestingly, Asians, on average, eat 20 grams of soy per day, whereas North Americans eat virtually none. It turns out that soy contains phytochemicals called isoflavones, which have been found to possess disease-preventing properties. Thus, North Americans should consider eating soy on a regular basis as a way of preventing fatigue and depression.

The following is taken from the editorial section of the local newspaper in Rockingham:

"In order to save a considerable amount of money, Rockingham's century-old town hall should be torn down and replaced by the larger and more energy-efficient building that some citizens have proposed. The old town hall is too small to comfortably accommodate the number of people who are employed by the town. In addition, it is very costly to heat the old hall in winter and cool it in summer. The new, larger building would be more energy efficient, costing less per square foot to heat and cool than the old hall. Furthermore, it would be possible to rent out some of the space in the new building, thereby generating income for the town of Rockingham."

Visit **www.ets.org** for a many more practice questions.

CHAPTER 11 HOMEWORK

1. Set up a study schedule for tackling the analytical writing section of the GRE. The best way is to simply practice writing essays that include the five critical components discussed in this chapter.

2. Try to sit down and write an essay for both topics at least twice a week. This will require a three-hour commitment per week. Can you work this into your study schedule? If you can do two of these essays twice a week for at least one month prior to taking the GRE, you will probably score high on the analytical writing section.

3. Consider whether you want to make a small investment in having ETS® assist you in preparing for the analytical writing section of the GRE. If you are in the online section for the "GRE General Test," you can click on "GRE Priced Test Preparation Materials" and select "Score It Now" to receive assistance. This is an online writing practice. The price is $13 for two essay submissions. Those who elect to make this purchase and receive this assistance may compose and submit essay responses online for scoring. Scores are received immediately. Users also have the opportunity to review sample responses and general suggestions for improving their essay writing skills and more.

CHAPTER 12

What to Do One
<u>Week Before the Exam</u>

Congratulations. You have made it to the week prior to your exam. Did you ever think that you would make it this far? Do you now wonder why you ever doubted yourself?

By now, you have either been diligent in your studies or not. Depending on how consistent you have been with your studying and practicing, you likely either feel a sense of confidence or discomfort right now. Conversely, even someone who has been preparing every day, six days a week for the last two months might feel some anxiety, particularly if that person experiences test anxiety.

Whatever the case may be for you up to this point, you have one week before you take your GRE General Test. This week is an important week. Up until now, if you have been following your study plan and working hard, you have built momentum. You are on a roll. Congratulations on your efforts and wish to assuage any nervousness you may feel by assuring you that your hard work and preparation will pay off and that you will score higher on the GRE than if you had not studied or prepared as hard as you did.

The most important thing to remember about this week is to not make any significant changes in your life. Do not abruptly start or end anything. The second most important aspect of getting through this week is to continue your study schedule. You must also take a little time out to take care of yourself and indulge in some relaxation. This will reset your brain.

Tip #76: Do not give up on your study schedule.

Face it: you have been training for a marathon. You are most likely tired. You might feel compelled to just chill out this week and forget about this pesky exam. Now, though, is not the time to abandon your GRE preparations. Continue to study. Continue to practice, practice, and practice. You are almost there. Do not give up now. If you suddenly discontinue your GRE preparations one week before the exam, you may run the risk of forgetting valuable information and strategies. Now is not the time to give up. Now is the time to dig in and kick it into high gear for one more week.

Conversely, while you should not give up on your study schedule, you do not need to increase it, either. Adding a significant number of hours to your current study schedule might overwhelm you. You do not want to feel overwhelmed or in panic mode one week before the exam. Now is the time to just keep doing what you have been doing all along– studying and practicing.

Tip #77: Do not begin a new routine, diet, or exercise plan.

Beginning a new routine, diet, or exercise plan can be challenging and stressful. While you have been studying for the GRE, and particularly now, you should not consider making any major changes or adjustments in your professional or social life. Avoid the following this week:

- Breaking up with a partner, significant other, or spouse

- Ending a friendship

- Looking for a new job

- Starting a new job

- Reducing your food intake

- Increasing your food intake

- Starting a new exercise program

- Discontinuing your current exercise program

Try and maintain the normal flow of your life. You do not have to over-think this point or avoid doing anything new altogether. The main point of the advice here is that making a dramatic adjustment to your life style can be challenging. You are about to face the exhilarating but somewhat elusive challenge of the GRE. You do not need to add any additional challenges or stressful situations to your life right now. Just keep things as they are. For example, if you normally drink coffee in the morning and afternoon, there is no reason to discontinue that practice. However, if you do not normally consume coffee or other forms of caffeine, now is not the time to suddenly begin. Your body is not used to this and you could experience unexpected, adverse reactions.

**Tip #78: Schedule something calming
and relaxing during the middle of the week.**

Depending on when your test date is, you should schedule something calming and relaxing about three to four days prior. Whatever you decide to indulge in should occur during one of your "off" days from studying. This will recharge you and reset your brain. It will also give you some much deserved and needed down time before you dig in for the final haul before your big test day. You would be ill-advised to engage in a relaxing and tranquilizing activity and then come home and study hard for several hours. Just choose a relaxing activity and enjoy it. Then come home and spend the rest of the evening relaxing.

There are several calming options available for to you to engage in, depending on your preferences and budget. Here are some examples of relaxing activities you could schedule a few days before your GRE. Similar to how restaurant reviewers indicate a number of dollar signs ($) to indicate how inexpensive or pricey a restaurant is, the same thing was done with the following suggestions. Again, you can pick and choose according to your preferences and budget.

- Lay out in the sun

- Go to the beach, dig your toes into the sand, and watch the waves

- Go to a local nature park and ride your bike, walk, or rollerblade

- Spend time with a friend

- Spend time with a loving family member

- Read a book you already have, but just never got around to reading

- Call someone you have not talked to in a long time and have an enjoyable conversation

- Do something you enjoy that you have not indulged in for some time, like dancing or painting

- Go to the bookstore, hang out, and just peruse all the magazines and books that interest you

- Rent a movie from the video store, kick back, and enjoy $

- Take a bubble bath $

- Go to a coffee shop or other food and beverage place you enjoy and treat yourself to something $

- Treat yourself to a meal out at a fairly inexpensive restaurant $

- Take a drive to a nearby city and explore $

- Treat yourself to something new but inexpensive, like a new shirt or CD $

- Get a pedicure $$$

- Get a manicure $$$

- Get a facial $$

- Get a massage $$$

- Schedule a half or full day at a spa $$$

- Play golf $$$

CHAPTER 12 HOMEWORK

1. Post your study plan for this week on your refrigerator, bathroom mirror, or somewhere that you will see it every day. Now is not the time to abandon your study plans.

2. Make sure that you schedule either one full day or one full evening off this week to indulge in your relaxation time to reset your brain and rejuvenate your spirit.

3. Choose a relaxing and calming activity and schedule it for your day or night off.

4. Enjoy whatever relaxing activity you choose. Do not go home that day and study. Take the rest of the day and/or the night off.

5. Commit to *not* making any dramatic changes in your life this week. No new boyfriends, girlfriends, pets, jobs, or drama. No new exercise routines. No increase in junk food. No decrease in healthy food. No sudden late nights at the library studying more than usual. Business as usual this week!

CHAPTER 13

What to Do the Night Before the Exam

The night before your exam is important. Do not give it more credit than it deserves, or you just might blow a fuse. It is important to do what makes you feel comfortable the night before the exam and it is important to get a good night's rest. If your test is early in the morning, it is also important to double-check your alarm. Other than that, you do not need to assign this evening more importance than any other day. There is no need to stay up the entire night studying– that would probably do you a grave disservice. Conversely, if you would like to study tonight as usual, there is no need to feel that you should not simply because it is the night before your exam.

> **Tip #79: Do whatever makes you feel comfortable, whether that is studying or just taking the night off.**

The night before your exam is extremely important but not the most significant evening of your entire life. As a previous GRE test taker, my personal advice is that you do whatever makes you feel comfortable, whether that is studying or just taking the night off.

I remember a time several years ago that I was participating in a GRE prep course. I had kept in contact with the teacher and he knew that my test was coming up the next day. He sent me an e-mail and told me to go out that night and just do something silly — like go see a crazy movie or do something fun. The reason he made this suggestion was to give my brain a rest.

Incidentally, I did not take his advice and felt grateful for that decision the next day. Personally, I just did not feel comfortable doing something goofy or fun the night before my GRE. What worked best for me was to have my usual study time of two to three hours. I spent the time taking a full-length practice exam from the ETS® software I had been sent when I registered for the GRE. After completing the test, scoring well and then reviewing all my notes, formulas and tips, I felt confident before going to bed. If I had gone out that night to see a goofy movie, I would have spent the entire evening thinking about how my preference was to study. I would have pondered how instead of watching a movie that I could have seen after the GRE, my desire was to review formulas, tips, and strategies instead. What worked best for me was to stay home and study the night before the test. Please note, though, I did not study any longer or harder than usual. It was business as usual for me.

You must do whatever feels comfortable for you. Everyone's personality is different. If you have a personality like mine, you will feel more comfortable staying home and studying. If you have a personality like my ex-GRE prep course teacher, you will likely want to go out and see a movie, go mini-golfing, or just goof off. There is no right or wrong decision in terms of what to do the night before your exam. Again, I strongly urge you to do what makes you feel comfortable and to ignore anyone's advice that indicates otherwise. No one else is going to go into the ETS® testing center for you tomorrow and take this exam. You are going to take the exam tomorrow, therefore you should do what makes you feel comfortable.

Tip #80: Get a good night's sleep!

Although you might be tempted to stay up the entire night studying for your exam, it is not a good idea. If you are anything like me, you will get the zany idea in your head that if you stay up all night and continue to jam formulas and tips into your head, you will perform more successfully the next day. In all likelihood, this hypothesis is not correct. If you have followed the procedures outlined in this book, your GRE preparations have steadily progressed over the course of a few months. There is nothing that you can do tonight to make or break your performance tomorrow. Whatever you have done up to this point will carry you through on your test performance tomorrow. If you stay up half of the night trying to memorize formulas that you did not bother to learn, or attempt to learn an entire set of vocabulary words, you will not be successful. It is too late to learn massive amounts of information for tomorrow's test.

The best thing to do is get a good night's sleep. Follow your normal sleep patterns, although other professionals might not agree with me. Some of your friends and family will tell you to hit the sack extra early and to try and pack in nine hours of shut-eye. Do you normally sleep nine hours per night? If you do not, it is not likely that this will suddenly occur the night before your exam. In fact, it is quite unlikely. Go to bed when you normally do, unless it is customary for you to sleep four hours a night, in which case you should try and get in at least a few more hours of sleep. There is no need to be overly dramatic and add or take away a significant amount of hours from your normal sleep pattern. Remember: You have been training for test day for a long time now. You are already prepared. Stick to business as usual.

Tip #81: Make sure your alarm is set properly and set two alarms if possible.

If you are scheduled to take your exam early in the morning, you should make sure that your alarm is properly set. If you have two alarms, set both of them. If you do not have two alarms, go out right now and purchase a second one. Then synchronize it with the other one and set it to the time that you need to wake up tomorrow morning.

This advice is not intended to make you feel anxious or worried. It is merely to remind you that tomorrow is an important day. Although you are ready and prepared with your tips, strategies, vocabulary list, and algebraic and geometrical formulas, none of this will do you any good if you oversleep and do not make it to your exam. Do not let something as foolish as oversleeping stand between you and the higher GRE score that you deserve.

If you decide to invest in a second alarm clock, there is no need to purchase anything extravagant or expensive. Just select the cheapest one. Then, go to bed and rest easy. Not only are you prepared for the exam, but you are now doubly prepared to wake up on time.

CHAPTER 13 HOMEWORK

1. Decide how *you* want to handle the night before your exam. What makes you feel comfortable? Do you want to study or go out? Ignore anyone and everyone's advice who tells you to do *anything* that makes you feel uncomfortable the night before your exam. Trust me: You need to do what makes you feel comfortable, as long as staying up all night studying is not included in those measures.

2. Unless you have unhealthy sleep habits and always go to bed at 3 a.m. and need to wake up at 6 a.m. tomorrow for your exam, go to bed at your usual time. Do not add or subtract a significant amount of hours from your usual sleep pattern.

3. If your exam is in the morning, set two alarm clocks. Make sure they are synchronized. Again, if you need to purchase a second alarm clock, go buy it now. The peace of mind will be well worth the $7 or $8 you spend on your second alarm clock.

4. Practice the anxiety reduction technique you selected earlier in the book before you go to bed. You may even wish to use it to lull yourself to sleep.

5. Go to bed with confidence. Know that you are prepared. You are ready for tomorrow. You have worked hard and have nothing to worry about. You are armed with several contingency plans in place. You have done everything that you could possibly do up until this moment.

Chapter 14

How to Handle Test Day

Handling test day may seem like the most stressful part of this entire process. It is the big day. It is your big day. You will be nervous about remembering all your vocabulary, reading comprehension skills, writing skills, mathematical and geometrical formulas, and the few tips and strategies that you have learned to use when you do not know how to answer a question. If, though, you have been practicing for the GRE on a regular basis, you have nothing to fear. Today should be just like any other day, except that today your scores count. Try to forget about your scores for a moment though. Remember that you have studied. You have prepared. You have practiced. Taking a full-length GRE is nothing new to you. You may have even been to the testing center by now. You know where it is. You know what it looks like. You know exactly what to expect.

At the beginning of this book, your GRE preparations were compared to marathon training. Remember: You have trained. You have on your running shoes. You know the marathon course; you are intricately familiar with it and have run it multiple times, even under timed conditions. The only difference about today is that when you finish your test, the computer is going to assign you a "score." Moreover, if you so desire, the computer is going to send your scores to the academic institutions of your choice. Nothing else about today is different.

Regardless, there are still a few things you can do to make your test day go even smoother.

Tip #82: Wake your body up in the morning.

This tip is especially important if your test is scheduled for the morning. "Waking up your body" with exercise may or may not be a regular part of your routine. Many people wake up every day, roll out of bed, take a shower and then proceed throughout the day. Or, right after you wake up, you can do some yoga and other stretching. It gets the blood flowing more fluently. The muscles start to wake up, and so does the mind.

Even if you do not normally engage in morning exercise, do something today. For those of you who have a regular routine, just stick to business as usual. Individuals who do not regularly exercise should not suddenly go for a jog, run, long walk, or take up yoga or Pilates. Just do some light stretching. You could also go for a short walk of about 10 minutes. Your goal is not to burn calories; it is simply to wake up your body and mind.

Tip #83: Consider whether caffeine is for you today.

We have previously talked about routines, including caffeine. Remember, it is still business as usual. Test day is no exception to this rule. If you normally drink coffee in the morning, have your coffee in the morning. If you do not drink coffee in the morning, do not suddenly go to the nearest coffee store, buy a gigantic cup of java and hope that it brings you a higher GRE score. More than likely, all that you will accomplish via the latter method is the onset of nervousness, restlessness and additional anxiety.

One other point to consider on caffeine is that if your routine is unhealthy or admittedly disruptive to your life, you should consider modifying it for today. For example, if your routine is to drink three cups of coffee in the morning after which you have to use the restroom three times an hour for the next four hours, this will not work for you today. Instead, just have one cup of coffee.

> ## Tip #84: Review (briefly) your formulas and flashcards before the test.

Stick to your guns on this one. There are plenty of people who will tell you to just go to bed early, then get up and cruise into the test center without reviewing a single aspect of the test. It is a good idea to conduct a brief review before the test. A brief review will "warm up" your brain. Remember how you warmed up your body in the morning? You need to warm up your brain as well. It needs to start thinking in GRE test taking terms before you sit down to the test.

There is no reason to go overboard, wake up early and spend hours looking at your formulas, flashcards and tips. Remember, you are simply attempting to bring your mind into the most clear and alert fashion possible. Also, reviewing your vocabulary flashcards, formulas and tips may prove useful when you sit down to take the test.

I will tell you a true story. The second time I took the GRE (to enter a Ph.D. program), I saw a vocabulary word on the test that I had just reviewed in my flashcards before I went in to take the test. The only means by which I was able to know the definition of the word and properly identify its antonym was through the brief review I had just conducted beforehand. While I might have studied this word multiple times before, seeing it just before the test helped me later. Likewise, there may be a mathematical or geometrical formula that you attempt to retrieve from your memory during the test. At first, you may have trouble. Then, it will suddenly come to mind because you just saw it during your brief review before you walked into the test center.

> ## Tip #85: Arrive at the test center at least 15 minutes earlier than your appointed time, with your photo identification.

When you received your test date confirmation from ETS®, you were probably instructed to arrive at the testing center early. Make sure that you do arrive at least 15 minutes prior to your GRE session. Ensure that you have your photo identification with you. Without it, you will be turned away. This will give you time to check in, get your locker, get a drink of water, and use the restroom right before the test. The last thing you want to do on your "big day" is sprint into the test center late and feel stressed about whether they will allow you to take the test. If you are late, you will probably not be allowed to take the test. Do not be late.

Conversely, do not arrive at the testing center excessively early. Doing so will only give you additional time to sit there with nothing to do except worry and wait. Such an action is neither healthy nor helpful. I made this mistake the first time I took the GRE. I arrived 40 minutes prior to my testing session. I had conducted my review in my car. Of course, as you know, you are not allowed to bring testing materials into the testing center. Therefore, after checking in, getting my locker, receiving my paperwork, getting a drink of water, and using the restroom, I still had about 20 minutes to kill. I had nothing to do but worry and wait. Those 20 minutes were agonizing. Do not arrive earlier than is necessary. You will regret it.

Tip #86: Say a prayer, do meditation, say positive affirmations, or whatever other techniques you find of comfort to you.

Prior to commencing your test, whether in the lobby or as you sit down in front of the computer, say a prayer, engage in a brief meditation, say a positive affirmation or whatever technique or practice makes you comfortable. If you previously selected an anxiety reduction technique, you may want to practice that. If you are of a religious or spiritual nature, you might elect to say a prayer or meditate. There is no "right" or "wrong" technique here; you may not want to do anything except take one, deep breath. Remember, this is your day and your race. It is all about you. Do what makes you feel comfortable but do not forget to take the time to engage in something that might alleviate your anxiety right before the test.

CHAPTER 14 HOMEWORK

1. Decide how you will "wake up your body" on test day. Remember to account for this extra time when setting your alarm clock the night before the test. You will need at least 10-15 minutes to do some light stretching, go for a walk or whatever activity you choose to bring your body into a state of alertness.

2. Decide on your caffeine plan for the day. If you normally drink coffee at home and have an early exam in the morning, set up your coffee machine the night before. Then, when you wake up in the morning, all you have to do is flip the switch. If you plan to stop somewhere for coffee prior to the test, remember to account for this in your schedule before arriving at the test center. Also, remember that you will not be allowed to bring food or drinks into the testing room. You can bring them to the testing center, but you will need to place any food or drink items in a secured locker.

3. Get prepared for your test day review the night prior. Put everything you need for a quick review in your car the night before the test. That way, if you have additional stress and anxiety on test day, you do not have to worry that you might forget your test review materials or flashcards.

4. Plan what time you will leave your house on test day. Then, plan to leave 10 minutes earlier than that.

CHAPTER 15

What to Do After the Test

I congratulate you in advance because I hope you read this chapter before you take your GRE so that you know what to do after. The "congratulations" is (of course) for taking your GRE. So much momentum and motivation has culminated in the moment when you finish the test. When you do answer that last question, however, do not "check out" mentally. You still have a bit of work to do. You also need to have some fun. As a previous test taker, I would like to point out a few things that you will want to know and remember right after you take your GRE.

Tip #87: Have your scores reported (unless you are absolutely certain that you bombed the test).

After you finish your test, you will be presented with two options. You can either have your scores reported to the four institutions of your choice, or you can opt not to have your scores reported. It is difficult, if not impossible, for me to advise you on whether to have your scores reported. Despite that, in most cases it is best to have your scores reported. What if you did better than you think? What if you feel that you bombed it, but you actually knocked it out of the ballpark? What if you did not do as well as you had hoped, but scored high enough to get into the institution of your choice? Also, since the schools to which you will send your application packet will only consider the GRE as one aspect of the admissions process, your GRE score will not "make" or "break" whether you make the cut. If, up to this point, you have worked hard, studied, and put forth the time and effort to prepare for this test, you deserve to know your score.

The following represent scenarios that present a case in which you should not have your scores reported:

- You are not adept with language or math skills and did not study for the GRE.

- You studied for the test less than 10 hours and do not have much proficiency in language or math skills.

- You are applying to a program that will weigh the verbal section of the GRE quite heavily and you did not recognize more than half of the words in the antonym and analogy sections and feel certain that you totally bombed that portion of the test.

- You are applying to a program that will weigh the math section of the GRE more significantly than the verbal section, and you were unable to compute the answers to several questions on the test and had to guess on most of them.

- Overall, you are more than certain that you completely bombed the entire test because you feel certain that you did not know the correct answer to the majority of the questions on the test.

Regarding the last point: Remember, this only applies if you are certain that you did not know the answer to *most* of the questions on the *entire* test. This would be an extremely rare case that would only apply to an individual with low writing, language, and math skills and who put in little to no study time. This does not apply to students who were nervous, steadily answered questions, and think they missed some but got some correct.

Do not make this a guessing game. Do not try and retrospectively tabulate how many questions you got right or wrong. You know what you brought to the table before you took the GRE. You know whether you took the time to study the structure of the GRE before taking it. You know what your language and math skills were before taking the exam. You know whether you created a study schedule and followed most of it or not. You know whether you studied two hours, 20 hours, or 200 hours for this test. You know the right thing to do. Most of the time, the right thing to do is at least reward yourself for all your hard work by finding out your score on the test.

> **Tip #88: Make sure to write down your scores on a piece of paper.**

After you decide to report your scores, write them down on one of the scratch pieces of paper that you were given before you started taking the test. The computer is *not* going to give you a print out of your verbal and math score; they will simply appear on the screen. You will not get an official report with your scores, including your score on the analytical writing section, for 10-15 business days. Also, remember, even if you write down your scores on a scratch piece of paper, the testing center may be required to confiscate that paper after your test. If that happens, make sure you transfer the scores onto a piece of paper that you have in your purse or wallet. If you do not have any paper to transfer your scores to; ask for something at the testing center. Do not leave the testing center without your scores.

Here are a few reasons why you should record your scores after the test:

- You will still be shaky and nervous after taking the test. You will attempt to remember your quantitative (math) and verbal scores later on but will not be able to do. The numbers will be precise and it is not likely that you will recall them later.

- You may want to recall the scores later because people will ask you how you did. If you have not written your scores down, the best answer you will be able to come up with is something like, "I do not remember my exact score; I know I got over 600 on the verbal section." Then, you will start obsessing about what your score actually was. Just write the scores down and then you will have them.

- Depending on the application deadlines of the schools and programs of your choice, you may need to send out your Master's or Ph.D. program application before you receive your official score report in the mail. For example, if you took the GRE on April 1 and you need to send out your application to one of the graduate schools of your choice by April 3, you will need to put your scores on the application. The institution will receive the verification of your scores later, via electronic means.

Tip #89: Regardless of your test score(s), go do something to celebrate your hard work in preparation of and taking this exam.

If you have not already learned this lesson in life, take note: It is worth celebrating the achievements and successes of your life. It takes guts to go into an ETS testing center and take an entire GRE under the timed and stressful circumstances involved. It takes even more courage and determination to adequately and appropriately prepare for the test, then go to the ETS test center and apply all your knowledge under timed circumstances. You have worked hard in preparation for this day. You should reward yourself and celebrate for preparing for and taking the GRE. If you scored as well as or better than you had hoped, you can add that to your reason for celebration. You should still celebrate, though, regardless of your score. Also, remember not to interpret or analyze your scores. Even if you did not score as well as you had hoped; you may still get into the program of your choice. Do not decide you do not deserve a celebration for any reason whatsoever. You did it. You walked into that test center and you took the GRE. Congratulations! Take at least a few hours off from your day to recognize this momentous occasion. Go treat yourself to lunch or dinner (depending on what time it is after you took the test). Buy yourself some ice cream. Go to a park. Go to the beach. Go home and take a nap. Buy a bottle of bubbly champagne for later (if you are old enough to of course)! Whatever you do, do not sell yourself short. Celebrate!

CHAPTER 15 HOMEWORK

1. Remember your plan to leave the testing center with your scores for the verbal and math sections in hand. You may be so anxious or excited after taking the test that you forget. Remind yourself the night prior.

2. Plan your celebration ahead of time. If you intend to go out with a friend, set up the meeting time at least a week ahead of time. If you plan anything else that requires an appointment, set up the time at least a week ahead of time. If your celebration plan does not require an appointment, you should at least decide on what activity you plan to enjoy. Rewarding yourself is an important part of this process. If you leave your "celebration" plans until after the test, you are likely to tell yourself, "Oh, I don't really feel like doing anything; I'll just go home and sit on the couch." Make sure you give credit where credit is due. You have worked hard up until this day, regardless of how your scores turned out.

Chapter 16

Score Reporting: Waiting and Wondering

Writing down your scores for the math and verbal sections should alleviate some of the "waiting and wondering" involved in the GRE scoring process. Although ETS does consider those scores which you receive at the ETS Center after your taking your test "unofficial," there are not any score reversals. Also, since I have taken the GRE twice, I can advise you that the scores I received from the ETS testing center and those received from ETS via U.S. mail never differed. Nonetheless, you have worked hard and may be anxiously awaiting your official GRE score report. Also, you may want to know how you performed on the analytical writing section of the test. The best thing to do is keep cool, store your records (scores) that you have in a safe place, and utilize the ETS Phone Score Reporting System if you get too impatient to wait for the mail.

> **Tip #90: Keep a record of the scores you wrote down for the math and verbal sections at the testing center.**

You took the time to write down your scores after you took the GRE. Do not lose the scores. I once made the mistake of carelessly throwing the scores somewhere in my car after taking the test. I was so excited and exhilarated that the test was over and that I had done well, that I was not careful with my scores. Later, when I wanted to refer back to the scores, I could not find them. They had fallen between the crack of my driver's seat and console. I was in a panic! I did eventually find them. Make sure you take care with your scores. Put them in your wallet after you take the test. Then, as soon as you get home, put them in your "GRE" test file. If you never created that file, as was previously advised in this book, create one today. You must put those scores in a safe place in case you need them for an application.

Tip #91: Wait at least 10-15 business days for your analytical writing scores to be processed.

It can take anywhere from 10-15 days for your analytical writing scores to be processed. None of your scores will be mailed to you without the inclusion of your analytical writing score. That is why you recorded your verbal and math scores after taking the test. You at least have those at your fingertips. Few institutions or departments weigh the analytical writing section of the GRE heavily. Remember, the GRE is only one aspect of the admissions process. The analytical writing section of the GRE is therefore only one factor of one aspect of your application packet.

Tip #92: Decide whether you want to wait for your scores to be mailed or if you want to pay to get them earlier over the phone.

If any of you are impatient like me and want to know your analytical writing scores before all your scores are mailed, you can call ETS and use the "Scores by Phone" Service. I did this on one occasion and received my analytical writing score before my official score report was mailed. Since I had scored a 6.0, it made my day and was worth the money I paid to get that score over the phone, as opposed to waiting for it to arrive in the mail. The fee to receive scores over the phone is $12.

Here is the information you will need if you opt to receive your scores by phone.

5. Call the appropriate phone number between 6:00 a.m. and 10:00 p.m., EST, 7 days a week.

    - **1-609-771-7290**

    - **1-888-GRE-SCORE (1-888-473-7267)**

        U.S., U.S. Territories, and Canada

    - 1-888-473-8333 (TTY)

According to ETS, you can only use these services if you call from a touch-tone phone, pay by credit card (American Express®, Discover®, JCB®, MasterCard®, or VISA®), and have tested in the last 5 years. You should wait for confirmation before you hang up.

2. Also, ETS requests that you have the following information ready when you place your call:

    - Registration Number, Social Security Number, or Confirmation Number

    - Test Date

    - Date of Birth

    - Institution Code(s)

    - Department Code(s)

> **Tip #93: Do not let your scores dictate your mood.**

The GRE is not a fun or easy test, nor is the preparation process for it free from problematic and challenging steps, either. While you are waiting, do not let any anxiety that may arise dictate your mood. Remember, what arrives in your mailbox in the next 10-15 days is a piece of paper. It will not make or break the rest of your life.

Also, remember that if you do not score as well as you would have liked to, you may still get accepted into the institution of your choice. Also, you can retake the test. That option will be discussed in the next chapter.

Conversely, if you expect to score as well as you had originally hoped, do not assume that this means you will be accepted to the Graduate Institution of your choice. In this respect, I do not mean to rain on anyone's parade. I do, though, want you to have a realistic outlook on the Graduate Admissions process. Gaining acceptance into an accredited graduate school is a competitive process. You may be compared with several people who have just as good a GPA and GRE score as you. If it comes down to you and another candidate, the admissions committee will have to look at other factors to make a decision. Stay focused on the admissions process though. If you have not yet written your admissions essay and procured your letters of recommendation—all aspects of the graduate admission process—make sure that you recognize the equal significance of those factors. If you have an application deadline coming up, you need to keep working toward gathering all the information, letters, and transcripts necessary for your packet. Do not assume that just because you scored well on the GRE you can let these other things slide or that you can just quickly churn out a half-hearted admissions essay.

The bottom line is to not let the unofficial scores you received at the ETS center or the official score report you are awaiting dictate your mood. It is all right for them to *affect* your mood; this is natural. Do not let them control your state of mind. They do not have that much power.

CHAPTER 16 HOMEWORK

1. Keep the scores you wrote down at the testing center in a safe place. If you already started your "GRE" test file, as advised earlier in this book, you can put your scores there. If you never started a GRE file, it is not too late. Just make sure you put your scores in a safe place where you can easily find them later on, in case you need them for an application.

2. Remember the scores by phone option if you need to verify your quantitative or verbal scores before your official score report comes in, or if you get anxious about your analytical writing score.

3. Remember: You have your scores; your scores do not have you. Do not let your GRE scores control your mood and life. The GRE is just a test. It is only one part of the graduate application process. You can take it up to five times per year. Relax.

CHAPTER 17

How to Handle Dissatisfactory Scores

If you already know after leaving the ETS® Center or receiving your official score report in the mail that your scores are dissatisfactory according to what you needed to achieve to gain admission into the college of your choice, there is no reason to overreact. Do not get so upset, angry, or discouraged over this that your mood prevents you from taking the next necessary steps. There are many people who do not score as well as they would have liked to when they first take the GRE. There are several reasons this could occur, including the following:

- You have text anxiety

- You faced a personal challenge of a serious nature during the GRE preparation process that distracted you from your studies

- You had an argument with your spouse or significant other the night before the test

- You overslept a bit on the morning of your test, scrambled to get ready and barely made it to the test center on time. Therefore, you never had the opportunity to review, which did not give you the confidence boost you needed to walk in the testing center and hit a home run

- You were so stressed and worried about the test (even if you do not have test anxiety) that you did not perform as well as you could have

- You did not study enough

Notice that none of these reasons indicate that you do not have the competency and wherewithal to score higher the next time you take the GRE. I had to take the GRE a second time to gain admission into a Ph.D. program. I successfully improved my scores. Remember that not scoring as high as you would have wished does not mean that you will not in the future. You must adopt a consciousness of success regarding this. You must have faith in yourself that you will do better next time.

> **Tip #94: Remember that ETS will allow you to retake the test once a month, up to a maximum of five times per year.**

The great news about dissatisfactory scores is that they can be improved. According to ETS®'s rules and regulations, you can retake the GRE once a month, up to a maximum of five times per year. Even though you may be discouraged about your scores, do not let your disheartened mood prevent you from taking advantage of the additional opportunities that ETS® offers for you to retake the test. You can still take four more shots at the score you want this year.

> **Tip #95: Plan another date to take the GRE.**

You should immediately plan the next date that you will take the GRE. Do not ruminate over your scores for a week, a month or any longer. Take action right away, while you have your GRE momentum in motion. You could take the GRE again as early as 30 days from the date you first took the test. Only you can determine: 1.) If 30 days is enough time for you to sufficiently prepare to retake the GRE — given whatever social, academic and familial obligations you have in the meantime; 2.) If you will actually prepare a study schedule and follow it within the next 30 days.

Be realistic with yourself. Let's say, for example, that you plan to take the GRE during a busy semester. Let's assume for the sake of this example that you receive dissatisfactory scores. In this scenario, the next 30 days a filled with high priority academics, and you have a test that accounts for 20 percent of your grade in a class. This might be a case in which you would not want to plan to retake the GRE within 30 days.

Keep the following in mind when planning your next GRE test date:

- You *should* plan to take the GRE again as soon as possible.

- You *should* keep your application deadlines in mind (as discussed previously) when determining the next date that you will retake the GRE. You may not be able to afford the luxury of waiting more than 30 days.

- You *should* be realistic about how much time and effort you will put into your second go-around with the GRE.

- You *should* assess your upcoming social and familial obligations over the next 30 days and determine which activities can be eliminated so that you can prepare to retake the GRE.

- You *should* plan another date to take the GRE.

- You *should not* decide to wallow in your disappointment and misery for an unspecified time and then decide when to retake the test after you "feel better."

- You *should not* decide that you cannot possibly do better if you retake the test and just decide not to take it again.

- You *should not* decide that you will "figure this all out" later because you need a break right now.

Tip #96: Register for the GRE again.

Now that you have determined your next GRE test date, do not waste any time. Register for the GRE again. You already know how to do this, since you have done it before. You can register over the phone or online. Make sure to get your confirmation number. Make a new (second, separate) file and label it "GRE Test 2." Put your confirmation number and any other important information about your second test date in that file.

Tip #97: Develop your study plan (like you did the first time around).

Refer back to Tip #35 in Chapter 5 to review the information about study plans. You might consider tweaking your study plan to prepare for your second GRE exam. If you did well on one section and not on the other, for example, you may want to study more in your weaker area than you did the first time around. Your study plan should still address all sections of the test, though: The quantitative, verbal reasoning, and analytical writing sections. Do not disregard the analytical writing section if you did well on it on your first GRE. Likewise, do not omit a study plan for either the verbal or math sections. You must study for all parts of the test. You can, though, give more time to a section that needs additional attention.

Tip #98: Repeat your study plan.

You will now follow your second study plan. If you followed your first study plan to the tee and did not score well on your first GRE, do not let that affect your mood or self-confidence for your second test. As previously stated, a multitude of reasons could be responsible for why you did not score as well as you had hoped. It may have nothing to do with your intelligence or capacity to score well; it could have everything to do with the stress and anxiety you experienced when you took the GRE for the first time. Conversely, if you did not adhere to your study plan the first time around, now is the time for a course correction. Determine to follow the plan, no matter what. Never underestimate the power of organization and a plan. Remember what I shared with you earlier: When I first sat down to write this book, I developed a plan that detailed how, when, and where I would write each section of this book. I determined when I would write how many words. Of course, unexpected circumstances occasionally arose and I did not get to write the 3,000 words I had planned to write for that day. Just imagine, though, if I needed to write 3,000 words a day and just goofed off for 6 days. That would have put me 18,000 words behind schedule. Make a plan and stick to it.

Tip #99: Take the test again.

Now that you have determined the date on which you will take your next GRE, registered for the GRE, prepared a study plan and followed through, you will simply find yourself back at the ETS® center to take the test again. Take the test in the same center in which you originally took the GRE. The reason for this recommendation is because you are already familiar with that testing center. You know how to get there. You know what the temperature is like. You know how the registration process there works. You know where the bathrooms and water fountains are. Why add anything new or stressful to your GRE re-take? Take the test again at the same testing center in which you originally took the GRE.

CHAPTER 17 HOMEWORK

1. If necessary, review your application deadlines again. Based on those dates, plan the next date to take the GRE.

2. Register for the GRE again. Make sure that you schedule your next test for at least 30 days after you took the first one.

3. Repeat the entire process again: Develop a study plan, follow through on it, practice, prepare and take the test again!

4. Keep your spirits up if you need to retake the GRE. Many people have to take it again; some people take it three of four times. Learn from your mistakes that you made the first time around, if you made any. Did you study enough? Did you curb your social life as was necessary to accomplish your study goals?

5. Continue to enlist the support of your friends, family, and spouse or significant other. Stay committed to the process and encourage them to help you stay focused.

CHAPTER 18

A Few Final Tips

**Tip #100: Study this list of helpful
information for taking the computer-based GRE.**

---

1. Be kind to yourself. Schedule your computer-based test for the time of day in which you are most alert and have the most energy.

2. Be practical. Do not try to fit a lot of other activities into the day you have scheduled your test. If possible, make your test session the major or only scheduled activity of that day.

3. Rest is best. Go to bed on time the night before the test. Actually, be conscious of getting enough rest and of eating right for at least a week before taking the test.

4. Use the tutorial for the computer-based test as many times as you can to accomplish the following tasks:

   a. Learning the directions for each type of question

   b. Reviewing the basic computer skills needed to take the test.

   c. Studying the fine points of the tutorial regarding how to select an answer, confirm an answer, and exit the test.

5. During the testing session, take a break between reviewing the tutorial

and taking the actual exam. Go outside and get some fresh air if possible. Be sure to attend to your personal needs so that you will not be distracted by biological functions.

6. Remember to budget your time. Do not spend either too much or too little time on any one question, and do not rush. Also, resist any temptation you may have not to finish the entire exam.

7. Think before you click the mouse. It is easy to make mistakes if you are under pressure.

8. Remember that seeing many difficult questions in a row is most likely an indication that you are doing extremely well on the test.

9. Watch for the five-minute warning.

10. Breathe!

**Tip #101: Study how to navigate the ETS®
Web site and other Web site locations.**

The ETS® Web site contains free practice questions and research materials that can give you valuable insights into how to take the GRE. You can also obtain testing dates and locations and register for the GRE online. It is a good idea to take a close look at this Web site and explore a few other Web sites that can help you learn the techniques you need to make a high score on the GRE or any other standardized test.

The ETS® homepage, **www.ets.org**, gives you a lot of information that you can use immediately. To start, there is a list of the standardized tests published by ETS®. Notice that the GRE is close to the top of the list of their tests, and that it is followed by iSkills, which is a literacy assessment. If you feel that you need more tutoring on the reading comprehension and vocabulary sections of the GRE than on the quantitative section, for example, you have just learned that you can find more test information on literacy and thus more practice questions to work with.

You might also notice that ETS® published the SAT®, a test that you have most likely already taken and passed. In addition, you will see the TOEFL®, TOEIC®, and TSE tests designed to measure the English Language skills of non-native speakers. The review sections of these tests may be just what you need to help you understand your own language even better than you already do.

NEWS

Notice the list of resources immediately beside the list of tests. If you click that link, you will be taken to a page containing news about ETS® test developments. Because the computer-based test has recently been revised, there is a lot of news about the changes in that format for 2008. Here is an example taken from the Web site in January 2008:

RESOURCES FOR HIGHER EDUCATION

NEWS

Revisions to the Computer-based GRE General Test in 2008

Contact: Tom Ewing: (609) 683-2803   tewing@ets.org

Princeton, N.J. (December 21, 2007) — Beginning in January 2008, the GRE Program will begin including reformatted reading passages in the verbal reasoning section of the computer-based GRE General Test. Currently, reading passages accompanying reading comprehension questions contain line numbers that reference specific parts of the passages. Those line numbers will be replaced with highlighting when necessary in order to focus the test taker on specific information in the passage.

The reformatted question types are part of the continuing improvements to the General Test. During this time, test takers may encounter both formats in their tests.

RESOURCES FOR HIGHER EDUCATION

"We believe the new format will help students more easily find the pertinent information in reading passages," explains David Payne, Associate Vice President in ETS®'s Higher Education Division. "The GRE Program will begin counting these questions types toward examinee scores as soon as an adequate sample of data from the operational testing environment is available."

Examples of the current and reformatted reading passages are available at **www.ets.org/newquestiontypes.html.**

In November 2007, two new question types were included in the verbal reasoning and quantitative reasoning sections of the computer-based GRE General Test.

Remember: No printed material can keep up with changes in an organization the way that a Web site can. To get information like that given above in a timely manner, you must go online.

GRE GENERAL TEST DESCRIPTION

When you navigate to the GRE Web page, you will see a brief statement describing the GRE, followed by a test taker's section. Here you will find an overview of the test, information for test takers with disabilities, a bulletin giving you even more (and always current) information about the GRE, the test registration page, practice tests, score reporting information, and other special sections as needed. Take some time to walk through each of these sections now.

Navigating to the GRE Details page will reveal links for all the sections listed above and more. You will discover point-by-point listings of what the general test measures and also who takes the test and why, where they can take it, and who accepts the GRE scores.

INFORMATION FOR TEST TAKERS WITH DISABILITIES

The second link on the GRE test takers page gives exceedingly important information for test takers with disabilities. The first and most important piece of information is that test takers who need accommodations cannot register online. If you need accommodations, you must contact ETS® Disability Services directly. Step-by-step directions for making contact and completing the registration process follow.

HOW TO GET A BULLETIN

The third link tells you how to get a bulletin, and navigating to that page will take you to a link for downloading a bulleting and give you instructions on how to receive a bulletin by mail. This page will also include information that might affect delivery of bulletins such as dates and times that the EAT distribution center will be closed.

SCORE REPORTS

Your test registration fee includes score delivery to up to four different institutions. If you take the paper-based test, you will fill out information about the score recipients during your registration process. If you take the computer-based test, you will designate the score recipients at the testing center. If you decide to add more score recipients at a later date, you will need to pay an additional fee for each new recipient.

Official score reports are sent directly to the named institutions. Your copy of the score report is for your information only and may not be used to fulfill college and university entrance requirements.

PRACTICE TESTS

"Free, official test preparation materials for the computer- and paper-based

GRE tests are available to anyone who registers for the GRE tests worldwide or who visits this Web site."

"GRE PowerPrep Software includes two computer-based GRE general tests, sample analytical writing topics, scored sample essays and reader commentary, test-taking strategies, a math review, and test tutorials. It is sent to individuals who register for the computer-based general test, or may be downloaded here."

As you can see from these two quotes, there is an abundance of practice and preparatory material available on the ETS® Web site. It also contains one full-length paper-based GRE General Test with test taking strategies and sample questions with fully explained answer selections.

OTHER WEB USEFUL LOCATIONS

Looking up Web sites through keyword searches is both fascinating and frustrating. It seems that Web sites are ever-changing and that you have no way of knowing the quality of information presented on many of them other than your own intuition. Although these things are true to some extent, your purpose in looking at Web sites other than at ETS® is to prepare yourself to take the GRE on a specific date, so you do not need to be concerned about how long the Web site will be maintained, and, if the information helps your review for that subject area, that is all you need to be concerned about. Due to the difficulty in determining the quality of individual Web sites, though, I am unable to provide a recommended list.

Some key terms that might help your search include:

KEY TERMS	
Explain analogy	Analogy Examples
Define analogy	Sample analogies
Define antonym	Antonym Samples

KEY TERMS	
Reading comprehension passages	Vocabulary building
Algebra tutorials	Geometry tutorials
Data analysis made easy	Interactive tutorials
What you need to know about....	How to study for....
How to prepare for standardized tests	Study skills strategies

Once you have identified the Web sites that seem most helpful to you in preparing for the GRE, bookmark them so that you can return to them as needed. Keep track of more Web sites than you think you will need in case any of them go inactive during your test preparation period, and list them according to how helpful you find them. Make this process part of your test preparation plan so that you will have dates and times to use each site and also an indication of how important to you each site is.

As a previous GRE test taker, the most useful resource I ever found out of all the books I read and Web sites I perused was the ETS® Web site, the resources it contains, as well as the software (with practice questions and practice tests).

CASE STUDY: FINAL ADVICE

Tricia Psarreas
The Brighter Writer
Founder/CEO
Lynn, Massachusetts

Before I started studying for the GRE, the only thing I knew was the horror stories I heard from others who took it. To avoid my own horror story, I bought the two largest GRE prep books I could find and started cramming.

After a week of studying for eight hours a day, I realized I wasn't retaining enough information. So I started studying for one hour a day and then I went through my vocabulary and formula lists for one hour a night. I checked off each word and formula I could perfectly define and kept going back until

---

CASE STUDY: FINAL ADVICE

I knew all of them. This studying method became my way of life for three months.

A week before the test, I stopped studying. I ran through words and formulas in my head without looking at any materials. The night before the exam, I relaxed and got plenty of sleep. When I woke up, I felt energized and ready. Three hours later, I walked into the testing center with a level of confidence I didn't know I had.

As it turned out, my studying methods worked. I got fantastic scores on all three parts of the GRE and I learned that the secret to doing well on the test was to know the basics. Analogies and equations don't mean anything if you don't know the words and formulas behind them. The GRE was proof that the building blocks of higher education are much like the building blocks of life. Focus on the basics and the rest will naturally make sense.

CHAPTER 18 HOMEWORK

1. Get familiar with the ETS® Web site, if you have not already done so. By now, you should have referred to the ETS® Web site several times to get additional practice questions for various portions of the test. If, though, for some reason, you have never visited the ETS® Web site. Do so now. Review whatever you can and learn whatever possible about the test.

2. Store any important contact phone numbers, Web sites, or e-mail addresses in your "GRE" test file.

Conclusion

Friends: We have reached the end of our journey. It has been a pleasure working with you and coaching you through the GRE process. I sincerely hope that you took the sentiments I expressed in the introduction of this book seriously. You can gain as much or as little as you want from this book. Some of you will read this book cover to cover, contemplate your life purpose, decide why you want to attend graduate school, choose schools and colleges to apply to, develop a study plan, follow through on it, fully prepare for the GRE using this book and other ETS® resources, then walk into the testing center and score high on the test. This is my hope for each person who reads this book. I also hope that if nothing else, you realize that the GRE is just a test. Like any other standardized test, it can be mastered with consistent time and effort. Study hard. Practice. Identify your weaknesses. Study more. Practice until you feel the exhilaration of the confidence this yields. Then, practice more. Always remember that *there are no shortcuts to the sweetest fruits in life,* including a high score on the GRE. The fruits you wish to bear, in this case, will only grow as the offspring of your sincere and persistent labor.

Good luck.

Bibliography

Britten, Rhonda. *Change Your Life in 30 Days: A Journey to Finding Your True Self.* New York: Penguin Group, 2004.

Boldt, Laurence G. *Zen and the Art of Making a Living: A Practical Guide to Creative Career Design.* New York: Penguin Group, 1991.

Donaldson, Ken. *Marry Yourself First: Saying "I Do" to a Life of Passion, Power and Purpose.* Seminole, Kenilee Ink, 2005.

Flickstein, Matthew. *Journey to the Center: A Meditation Workbook.* Somerville: Wisdom Publications, 2006.

Maslow, Abraham H. *Motivation and Personality,* 3rd edition. New York: Harper & Row, Publishers, Inc, 1954.

Milligan, Mark, "What are 'Colloidal Mineral Supplements' and Where do They Come From?" Utah Geological Survey, **http://geology.utah.gov/surveynotes/gladasked/gladcoll.htm**. Salt Lake City, 2008.

About the Author

Angela Eward-Mangione is currently a Ph.D. student in the English Department at the University of South Florida. She intends to focus her doctoral dissertation on suicide in Shakespearean drama. In conjunction with other teachers and professionals, Angela intends to use her research for suicide and homicide-suicide prevention efforts in the national community at large. She hopes to publish her doctoral dissertation and also aims for her research material to be utilized in middle and high schools throughout the country for suicide and homicide-suicide prevention efforts.

Angela received a bachelor's degree in English (American and British Literature), a graduate certificate in Comparative Literature/Interdisciplinary Studies, and a master's degree in Liberal Arts from a nationally recognized, research one university. She was also awarded a 6.0 — the highest possible score — and a 96th percentile ranking (nationwide) on the analytical writing section of the Graduate Record Examination (GRE). Previously, Angela served as a Guest Lecturer for the analytical writing section of the GRE at the University of South Florida's Continuing Education Division. She is currently a part-time instructor at a community college in Florida.

Angela is also a writer and editor. She started in 2005 with only a dream, a vision, and a firm commitment. Since then, Angela has had articles published in local, regional, and national publications. She has also authored articles for various online media sources and has served as the managing editor for a regional health and wellness publication since 2005.

Index